everyday raw

Matthew Kenney

photography by Miha Matei

Gibbs Smith, Publisher
TO ENRICH AND INSPIRE HUMANKIND
Salt Lake City | Charleston | Santa Fe | Santa Barbara

First Edition
12 11 10   12 11 10 9 8

Text © 2008 Matthew Kenney
Photographs © 2008 Miha Matei

Published by
Gibbs Smith, Publisher
P.O. Box 667
Layton, Utah 84041

Orders: 1.800.835.4993
www.gibbs-smith.com

Designed by Debra McQuiston
Printed and bound in Hong Kong

Library of Congress Cataloging-in-Publication Data

Kenney, Matthew.
  Everyday raw / Matthew Kenney ; photographs by Miha Matei. — 1st ed.
    p. cm.
  ISBN-13: 978-1-4236-0207-1
  ISBN-10: 1-4236-0207-2
  1. Vegetarian cookery. 2. Raw foods. I. Title.

TX837.K464 2008
641.5'636—dc22
                          2007038614

to liz, my inspiration

CONTE

introduction

Raw food is a miracle—it is so simple and obvious that we have made it complicated in order to find its core again. It is full of flavor, vibrant, and colorful, and great for our health. It is also challenging to prepare properly, because everything must be made from whole, fresh, and preferably organic ingredients, none of which may be heated above 118 degrees. As a result, the growing popularity of the lifestyle has bred many complex recipes and techniques, all with the goal of creating "gourmet" raw food. It is in our nature to experiment and, given the limitations involved when staying raw, the bar has been set high. In fact, I am one of the guilty ones, not only having opened several upscale raw cafes and restaurants in Manhattan, but also planning new ones in Miami and even India. But, those will be restaurants, with restaurant

food, and a large staff whose sole mission is to prepare amazing meals. At home, I am like everyone else, working alone in the kitchen with a very limited amount of time on my hands. I love to prepare complex meals for dinner parties and friends when I can, but that is not often these days. In my day-to-day life, I have a far smaller window in which to put together recipes. Still, being a chef, I can't suppress my desire to have great tasting foods on a daily basis. When I began eating raw food a few years ago, I also had to relearn all of my domestic culinary secrets, as I had done in my previous pre-vegan life. Those secrets are what allow me to eat well and creatively at home, but with far less work. The type of raw food that is best at home is unfussy and is made up of very satisfying ingredients, with far fewer components and fewer steps;

a lot of wow, a lot of simplicity

and it's easier to prepare in a shorter amount of time. Everyday raw food does not necessarily translate to simple—for better or worse, raw food will never be as easy as opening a can or popping something in the microwave. That comes with the territory when you are committed to a life of fresh fruits and vegetables. It is simply a good amount of work (or pleasure, depending on how you qualify it). But there are ways to streamline the challenge, and that is what this book is about—preparing restaurant-quality flavors in less time.

The recipes in this book also recognize the "lifestyle" factor involved in raw food. At a restaurant, the menu may be about elaborate creations, but at home, it is often preferable to have a smoothie or snack rather than a meal. For that reason, I have added a large number of my favorite smoothies and juices—many that have enough nutrition and energy in them to carry you all afternoon. There are also several component recipes that I like to call building blocks, or supporting characters. Added to any dish, they can quickly elevate it from something ordinary to something special.

You should always look at these recipes as a road map only—they can be adjusted, substitutions can be made, or components can be added to something else. The goal is to provide you with enough information and ideas to help with your day-to-day raw life. Keep it simple, fresh, organic, real, and delicious.

my philosophy

Although my food preferences have changed dramatically over the years, my culinary influences have not. Many years ago, the staff at my first restaurant used to make fun of how often I would use the words "clean" and "sexy" to describe how I wanted our food to be presented. I haven't wavered in my preferences on that level: I like food that is somewhat light, or lighter than usual, and very intensely flavored, yet not muddled with too many components. If an ingredient does not have a real purpose in a recipe, I prefer to leave it out.

The far most important element of raw food, or any food for that matter, is the sourcing of high quality, seasonal, local when possible, organic ingredients. Without them, you are already limiting your chances of preparing great, healthy food.

Having traveled extensively in the Mediterranean, I am strongly influenced by its cuisine, which is very seasonal, vibrant, and based on many ingredients that I still love today: olive oil, tomatoes, green vegetables, fresh fruits, spices, and nuts. Little did I know what a large role those part-time components would eventually play in my culinary pursuits.

Raw food is, by its own nature, very unique and without the tradition of other cuisines. In order to keep it somewhat grounded, I firmly believe in respecting cultural influences—for example, if we are preparing an Indian-inspired recipe, I work hard to keep the flavors as they would be in that cuisine, rather than also introduce a Thai ingredient. Although my first cookbook made liberal use of garlic, onions, and shallots, I have since gotten away from using too much of any of those. As I transitioned into raw foods, I also began paying more attention to how they made me feel and how they are digested. This is a personal philosophy; and even though we do use some of these ingredients, they are not automatically added to a dish and are only used when I feel that they add immeasurably to the recipe.

The far most important element of raw food, or any food for that matter, is the sourcing of high quality, seasonal, local when possible, organic ingredients. Without them, you are already limiting your chances of preparing great, healthy food. I was fortunate to grow up on the coast of Maine, with a garden in the backyard and an ocean in the front. It taught me a lot about seasonality, and the respect I have for seasonal ingredients is stronger than ever. I prefer to purchase ingredients that have not been on an airplane if possible. In the best world, I would like to eat food that never made its way into a refrigerator. But that will be another day—for now, I simply would like to emphasize that the quality of ingredients is critical. With raw food, we do rely on many ingredients that come from afar,

keep it simple and enjoy!

like young Thai coconuts. At the moment, they are invaluable. In the future, I do envision a raw cuisine that makes less use of some of these ingredients, but for now, enjoy them!

A frequent comment from people who are interested in preparing raw food is that it requires a lot of special equipment. That is not really the case. If I were living in a climate that was "raw food friendly" and ever decided to build a new home from the ground up, it would not have a traditional oven and stove, but rather a big stone and marble counter, with one small dehydrator, a couple of blenders, good sharp knives, an oak cutting board, a mandoline (slicer), and a food processor. Compare that to a gas or electric range, an exhaust fan, and numerous other gadgets. It is quite simple—but different. A dehydrator costs just over $200. Buy one instead of a microwave and preserve your food's nutrients rather than destroy them. All in all, the raw kitchen is very easy to put together and maintain.

Finally, just think freely. Experiment—mix and match. It all works in the end and what doesn't is still good for you. I learned the hard way, by trying to get too creative in the beginning. Now I know—keep it simple.

how to use this book

I hope that these recipes will make it easier for you to have access to high quality, delicious raw food in your home, without the stress often associated with challenging dishes, and without the disappointing results of those that appear easy. In the end, it has to be good or it is not worth the savings of time and effort.

The best way to use this book is to read it—in its entirety. If you like, prepare the recipes just as I have presented them. But if you are feeling a little more experimental, try taking the components (a sauce here, a technique there) and create your own cuisine. Mix and match, adjust, tailor to your own desires.

Many of these recipes are very simple and can be done in a short amount of time. Others do require more time. Save those for a weekend or for a period when you'll be home a lot. Once you get used to juggling the prepping, soaking, and dehydrating, it won't seem complex at all.

Most importantly, just keep it simple. Enjoy.

everyday handbook

Of course raw food has been around forever. Yet it is only in recent years that it has been elevated on a culinary level, celebrated in cookbooks and lifestyle magazines, and exposed in detail in newspaper articles around the globe. In the past three or four years particularly, that coverage has been not only widespread but also very informative. By now, most of us realize that heating foods above 118 degrees does destroy valuable enzymes and nutrients, and that in most cases the raw food lifestyle refers to one that is not only uncooked but also vegan, organic when possible, and that employs some pretty interesting preparation techniques. In writing this book, I felt that now is the time to forego repeating

that tried-and-true information and rather to focus my energies on developing the compelling flavors unique to raw cuisine with a little less process. Until the day arrives when every neighborhood offers up a "raw market," with presoaked and dehydrated almonds, freshly churned Thai coconut ice creams, and prepared macadamia hummus with sprouted crackers on their shelves, there are certain steps we can't avoid. The good news is that once we become accustomed to some of the longer but unavoidable steps to raw, we really are able to streamline things. A basic understanding of necessary equipment, techniques, and ingredients are all that is needed to begin the journey.

tools of the trade

Most of us have a variety of kitchen tools that will translate well to raw food preparation. Every well-equipped kitchen should include a high quality, very sharp knife. I like to work with a light Japanese chef's knife from Korin, or a Global. Global also makes a utility knife, slightly larger than a paring knife, which fills multiple roles. A cleaver is a necessary tool in working with the Thai coconuts. A Japanese mandoline, fine mesh strainer, cutting board, and measuring cups are useful every day. A good blender, preferably a Vita-Mix, is invaluable, whether it be used for smoothies, soups, or sauces. I have blended more in the last five years with raw food than in all previous years combined. Although a blender may be used for food processing, it is not optimal. Blending is a process used to do just that—to fully blend ingredients together, to emulsify them. Food processors (my favorite is the Cuisinart) are better for mixing ingredients, and preparing crusts, flours, pestos, or anything that will still retain some texture. Both the blender and the food processor are well used in the preparation of raw foods.

Much is said about the dehydrator in this and other raw food cookbooks. You can certainly live without it: use an oven at the lowest setting with its door propped open, or go back to nature and lay your foods in the sun. But the truth is, dehydrators are inexpensive and easy to use, and fulfill a very important role in creative raw food recipes. Excalibur seems to be the most common and most useful at the moment.

key products

The star ingredients of raw food include fruits, vegetables, nuts, seeds, and sprouted grains. The supporting cast is made up of oils, spices, and other condiments. Shopping

The star ingredients of raw food include fruits, vegetables, nuts, seeds, and sprouted grains. The supporting cast is made up of oils, spices, and other condiments.

for raw food is actually very easy—regardless of how large your market is, you can automatically pass over the meat, poultry, fish, dairy, pastry, and prepared food departments, forego anything from a can or that has been pasteurized or cooked, and skip the candy, cookies, and gum. In fact, a visit to two sections of a market usually covers a raw food shopping expedition: the fresh produce section and the dry goods section. Although I prefer not to subscribe to rules in general (if I had, its doubtful I would have ever shifted my career as a chef from cooked to raw), there are three rules that I really do adhere to whenever possible. One word defines each of them: *Seasonal, Sustainable,* and *Local.* The premise is about as natural a one as there is and also another subject that has been well covered. For me, sourcing produce in its peak season, from a local organic source, is as fulfilling as the preparation or enjoyment of the food itself.

With raw foods, there are a number of ingredients that are simply not available locally, especially for those in cooler climates. Young Thai coconuts are a preferred ingredient; I love them and still can't imagine many dishes without them. There are a number of tropical fruits that work well in smoothies and dressings that are usually shipped from afar. Spices travel a long distance. Still, if you source as many products locally and seasonally as you can, you will find great rewards in the process.

skill set

Enjoying the preparation of raw foods is a little easier, perhaps a little less stressful, and definitely not as intense as cooking with high heat. I have found that many people with limited cooking experience are quite successful with raw food recipes. The most important thing to bring to the kitchen is patience, which may be needed for a somewhat challenging recipe, a stubborn blender, and, of course, those soaking nuts and the slow process of dehydrating. The best advice I can offer in the kitchen is that you work in an organized fashion: keep knives sharp, ingredients well stored and rotated, equipment clean and in good working order. Finally, work with an open mind with the recipes—your discovery may be the next great raw food dish!

blended & squeezed

Smoothies and juices are the undisputed leader in the raw food lifestyle. Some people indulge in their favorite recipe in the morning, rely on green juice every afternoon, and sip coconut water throughout the day. I prefer all of the above. Juices and smoothies are easy to prepare and are the best way to pack large amounts of nutrition into one, easy-to-consume package. Many of them also have a fun, exotic element that makes them even more appealing.

the blue green

Over the years, I have become more and more interested in green smoothies and other unique combinations. This is one of my favorites. Blue green algae is one of the most nutritious foods on the planet—it provides clarity and immunity, and the taste is surprisingly subtle when combined with the richness of coconut. Its color is very unique as well.

2 cups young coconut meat
2 teaspoons extra virgin coconut oil
4 teaspoons blue green algae
1/4 cup agave

12 leaves fresh mint
3 cups coconut water
1 teaspoon vanilla
1 pinch sea salt

Blend all ingredients in Vita-Mix on high for 30–40 seconds. SERVES 2

immunity

Acai is not only very trendy, with its unique pungent fruitiness, but is incredibly high in antioxidants. Here, the South American miracle fruit is paired with our own North American antioxidant star, the blueberry.

1 1/2 cups frozen banana
1 packet (100g) frozen Acai
1 cup frozen blueberries

2 cups coconut water
1 teaspoon vanilla
1 pinch sea salt

Blend all ingredients in Vita-Mix on high for 30–40 seconds. SERVES 2

the blue green

almond milk

Nut milks are an invaluable ingredient in raw food preparation. We use them for creamy smoothies when sweetened, but you can also eliminate the agave and use them as a base for a sauce or purée.

1 cup almonds, soaked 4–6 hours
4 cups water
2 tablespoons extra virgin coconut oil

1 teaspoon lecithin
1/4 cup agave
1 teaspoon vanilla
1 pinch sea salt

Blend all ingredients in Vita-Mix on high for at least one minute. Strain through a chinois, nut milk bag, or cheesecloth; use a spoon to push as much liquid through as possible. Serve or store in refrigerator up to 2 days. YIELD 1 QUART

> " Nut milks are very easy to make and totally nutritious, with no hormones or antibiotics. They will keep 2 days in a covered container in the refrigerator. If they separate, just give them a good shaking. "

brazil nut milk

The high fat content and rich, unusual flavor of Brazil nuts work perfectly in this full-bodied recipe. This milk is also excellent as a cream—simply reduce the amount of water to 2 cups.

1 cup Brazil nuts, soaked 4–6 hours
4 cups water
2 tablespoons extra virgin coconut oil

1 teaspoon lecithin
1/4 cup agave
1 teaspoon vanilla extract
1 pinch sea salt

Blend all ingredients in Vita-Mix on high for at least one minute. Strain through a chinois, nut milk bag, or cheesecloth; use a spoon to push as much liquid through as possible. Serve or store in refrigerator up to 3 days. YIELD 1 QUART

almond milk

triple c

This is my favorite morning smoothie—it's refreshing enough to be a wake-up beverage, but rich enough to keep me going all afternoon if I have a busy day. Be careful with the cayenne, but use enough to enjoy it. It's part of the wake-up call!

1/2 cup goji berries
2 1/2 cups frozen mango
1/2 cup young coconut meat

6–8 oranges, juiced
2 pinches cayenne (optional)
1 pinch sea salt

Blend all ingredients in Vita-Mix on high for 30–40 seconds. SERVES 4

chocolate-cherry

With the recent availability of the cacao nibs, I have slowly tried to get away from using processed cocoa powder, which many raw food establishments still favor. The cacao bean is somewhat of an acquired taste, but once you acquire it, you'll crave it endlessly.

2 cups frozen cherries
2 cups frozen banana (or 2 fresh bananas)
1/4 cup cacao nibs

1 cup coconut water
2 tablespoons agave
1 teaspoon vanilla
1 pinch sea salt

Blend all ingredients in Vita-Mix on high for 30–40 seconds. SERVES 4

vanilla–e

The vanilla bean is one of the world's food miracles. The exotic aroma alone is enough to make me hungry. We kept this recipe neutral to let the vanilla essence come through, although you can feel free to add some mango or papaya.

4 cups frozen banana
4 teaspoons vanilla extract
1/2 vanilla bean, scraped

2 tablespoons tocotrienols
2 cups Almond Milk (see recipe page 24)
1 pinch sea salt

Blend all ingredients in Vita-Mix on high for 30–40 seconds. SERVES 4

> "Tocotrienols are a powder supplement in the vitamin E family and are available in most health food stores."

the classic

Strawberries and bananas have been a great combination since they were married in yogurt flavors years ago. This is an easy recipe to prepare and one that will please nearly everyone.

5 cups frozen strawberries
2 cups frozen banana
1 1/2 cups Almond Milk (see recipe page 24)

Blend all ingredients in Vita-Mix on high for 30–40 seconds. SERVES 4

vanilla–e

banana almond butter cup

I do my best to avoid using ice or water in smoothies, opting instead to freeze some component of the recipe, which intensifies flavors, while keeping the smoothie cool and refreshing. Whenever bananas are becoming very ripe, chop them up and pack them in ziplock bags in the freezer until you are ready to use them.

4 cups frozen banana
1/2 cup cacao nibs

1/4 teaspoon cinnamon
2 cups Almond Milk (see recipe page 24)
1/4 cup agave

Blend all ingredients in Vita-Mix on high for 30–40 seconds. SERVES 4

mango raspberry

When blackberries are in season, use them in place of raspberries in this great recipe.

3 cups frozen mango
2 cups frozen raspberries

2 cups Almond Milk (see recipe page 24)
1 teaspoon vanilla
1 pinch sea salt

Blend all ingredients in Vita-Mix on high for 30–40 seconds. SERVES 2

mint cacao cooler

This refreshing smoothie is more like a milkshake and is filling enough to have on its own as a light, decadent lunch.

1/2 cup young coconut meat
1/4 cup agave
1/2 vanilla bean, scraped

1/4 cup cacao nibs or cacao powder
2 cups Almond Milk (see recipe page 24)
10 fresh mint leaves

Blend all ingredients in Vita-Mix on high for 30–40 seconds. SERVES 2

banana almond butter cup

the muscle

There are so many great vegan sources for protein, and hemp is among the best. It also has a very nutty flavor that works well with the earthy flavor of pear and smoky mesquite in this recipe.

5 fresh pears, cut in quarters and cored
1 teaspoon cinnamon
2 tablespoons hemp protein
2 tablespoons mesquite pod meal

2 cups Almond Milk (see recipe page 24)
2 tablespoons agave
1 teaspoon vanilla
1 pinch sea salt

Blend all ingredients in Vita-Mix on high for 30–40 seconds. SERVES 4

> Ground from the bean pods of the wild mesquite tree, mesquite pod meal is very nutritious and can also be used in salads. Most upscale health food stores carry it.

best smoothie

This has a similar flavor to a piña colada and is an easy recipe to add additional ingredients to.

4 cups frozen pineapple chunks
1 cup young coconut meat
2 tablespoons agave

20 fresh mint leaves
2 cups coconut water
1 teaspoon vanilla
1 pinch sea salt

Blend all ingredients in Vita-Mix on high for 30–40 seconds. SERVES 4

the muscle

raspberry-agave lemonade

This is an excellent summer drink, appreciated for its look alone. But it actually tastes great, too. In a nice glass, it can be a very elegant-looking beverage for an upscale luncheon.

3 cups water
1 cup lemon juice

$1/2$ cup agave
8–10 frozen raspberries

Mix water, lemon juice, and agave together. Chill well; serve in tall glasses. Add 4 to 5 frozen raspberries to each before serving. SERVES 2

hot ancho cacao

In one of my earlier cafes, the landlord was slow to give us heat. The resourceful chef, Justin, created this recipe. We had no ovens or stoves, so he simply left it in the blender long enough for it to get hot. It is hauntingly spicy and kept us very warm.

4 cups Brazil Nut Milk (see recipe page 24)
$1/2$ cup cacao nibs
1 tablespoon cocoa powder
2 tablespoons maple powder

1 teaspoon ancho chile powder
$1/2$ teaspoon cinnamon
2 tablespoons maple syrup
3 teaspoons hazelnut extract

Blend all ingredients in Vita-Mix on high for 10–15 minutes until steaming hot. Place in a thermos or air-pot. Swish around before serving to avoid having sediment on the bottom. SERVES 4

sweet green juice

Green Juice is simply one of the finest things you can offer your body. It is a great replenishment after a vigorous run or yoga session and restores the body's balance quickly and efficiently.

2 cucumbers
2 carrots
2 apples
1/2 cup parsley

1/2 cup mint
1 stalk celery
1/2-inch piece ginger
1 lemon, peeled

Push all ingredients through juicer. SERVES 2

" Remember to always use
organic produce, especially when
you'll be juicing the peel, skin, or seeds. "

grapefruit cleanser

The grapefruit in this recipe lightens the juiced kale, making it not only easier to drink but very refreshing.

3 grapefruits, peeled
2 apples

2 limes, peeled
3 stalks kale

Push all ingredients through juicer. SERVES 2

snacks

Let's face it—snacking is fun and with all the time
we spend commuting and traveling, it's important to
always have handy treats nearby. These recipes are

some of my favorite ways to keep satiated throughout the day. And, they are so natural, that even the chipmunks that visit my place in Maine love them as well.

citrus maple granola

This recipe has too many potential variables to name; but to give an idea, it is easy to interchange the apple with a pear or replace any of the dried fruits with others. It is a granola that is great eaten as a snack or for breakfast with nut milk. It also works well on top of ice cream or pudding.

3/4 cup maple syrup
1 apple, peeled, cored, and chopped
2 1/4 teaspoons vanilla extract
2 1/4 teaspoons cinnamon
3/4 teaspoon sea salt
2 tablespoons fresh orange juice
1 tablespoon orange zest

1 tablespoon lemon zest
1 1/2 cups almonds, soaked 6–8 hours
1 1/2 cups walnuts, soaked 6–8 hours
1 1/2 cups pecans, soaked 6–8 hours
1 cup pumpkin seeds
1 cup raisins
1 cup dried cranberries

Mix maple syrup, apple, vanilla, cinnamon, sea salt, orange juice, and orange and lemon zests in a food processor until chunky. The mixture should be in very small pieces but not puréed. Pour into a large bowl. Set aside. Grind nuts in food processor until chunky. Add to bowl. Stir in pumpkin seeds, raisins, and dried cranberries, and mix all ingredients until very well combined. Crumble into larger pieces on dehydrator screens and dehydrate at 115 degrees for 36–48 hours, until crunchy. YIELD 2 QUARTS

mixed candied nuts

There are many uses for the various dehydrated recipes we prepare. These nuts are also used in our chocolate brownie and help make a great tart crust when crumbled into an almond flour base.

4 3/4 cups walnut halves, soaked 6–8 hours
4 cups pecan halves, soaked 6–8 hours
4 cups almonds, soaked 6–8 hours
1/2 cup + 2 tablespoons maple syrup

1 teaspoon vanilla extract
1/2 tablespoon sea salt
1 1/2 tablespoons cinnamon
1 1/2 cups maple powder

Dehydrate nuts 24 hours. In a large bowl, coat dehydrated nuts in maple syrup. Add vanilla, salt, cinnamon, and maple powder, and stir until well coated. Dehydrate on screens for 48 hours. YIELD 3 QUARTS

curried cashews

These cashews make an excellent snack on their own, but also work well chopped and added to a green salad or sprinkled over many of our Indian and Asian dishes for added texture.

6½ cups cashews, soaked 1–2 hours, drained, and
  dehydrated 48 hours
2½ tablespoons agave
¼ cup maple syrup

2 teaspoons curry powder
½ teaspoon cayenne powder
1¾ teaspoons sea salt

In a large bowl, coat dehydrated nuts with agave and maple syrup. Add curry, cayenne, and salt. Mix until well coated. Spread on screens; dehydrate for 2 days. Transfer cashews to a large bowl and separate by hand. Return to dehydrator screens and dehydrate 2 more days. YIELD 1½ QUARTS

blueberry-almond
granola bar

This is a far cry from the Quaker Oat granola bars I used to eat on camping trips in Maine when I was a kid, but they fulfill the same need for a quick on-the-go snack that is filling enough to keep you going during a busy day.

8 cups frozen blueberries, divided
2 cups Almond Crumbs (see recipe page 44)
1 cup cashew pieces
1 cup walnut pieces
½ cup sunflower seeds
¼ cup hemp seeds

¼ cup golden flax seeds, soaked for 2 hours and drained
1 cup agave
2 teaspoons vanilla extract
2 teaspoons almond extract
1 teaspoon lemon zest, finely chopped
½ teaspoon sea salt

Line a half sheet pan with parchment paper. Pour 3 cups of the frozen blueberries on the sheet pan. Lay another half sheet pan in bottom of dehydrator to catch any falling liquid. Dehydrate 8–9 hours. In a large bowl, mix dehydrated blueberries and remaining ingredients together until they are evenly incorporated. Spread mixture evenly in 2 parchment-lined half sheet pans and press firmly. Dehydrate overnight. Loosen from all sides of pan and turn out onto cutting board. Trim edges and cut into bars, 32 bars per half sheet pan. Return to dehydrator screens and dehydrate overnight. YIELD 64 BARS

raspberry vanilla-almond granola

This addictive recipe is best suited for summer when berries are at their peak, and you are interested in a brighter, lighter version of granola. The red flecks give it a nice vibrancy, and it is great with any nut milk or on ice cream as a dessert.

4 cups fresh raspberries
2 cups sunflower seeds, soaked 8–12 hours
3 cups pecans, soaked 8–12 hours
6 cups almonds, soaked 8–12 hours
1 1/2 cups maple syrup
1/2 cup date paste

2 pears, peeled, cored, and chopped
1 1/2 tablespoons vanilla extract
1 vanilla bean, scraped
1 tablespoon almond extract
1 1/2 teaspoons sea salt
1/4 cup ginger juice
2 tablespoons lime zest

Place raspberries and sunflower seeds in a large bowl; set aside. Process pecans and almonds in food processor until chunky; do not overprocess. Add to raspberries and sunflower seeds. Process all remaining ingredients in food processor until chunky; do not overprocess. Add to bowl and mix until ingredients are well combined. Crumble evenly over dehydrator screens. Dehydrate 48 hours, or until crisp. YIELD 3 QUARTS

chili-lime macadamia nuts

There are two things that I eat nearly every day of the year. The first is a lemon in water, which I start my day with, and the second is the macadamia, which I have been obsessed with since my first trip to Hawaii many years ago. I can't imagine traveling without a good amount of these in my bag.

6 1/2 cups macadamia nuts, soaked 1–2 hours, drained, and dehydrated 48 hours
1/4 cup maple syrup
1/2 cup agave

1 1/2 tablespoons lime juice
1 1/2 tablespoons lime zest
2 tablespoons chili powder
1/2 teaspoon cayenne powder
2 teaspoons sea salt

Coat dehydrated nuts with remaining ingredients in a large bowl. Transfer to dehydrator screens and dehydrate for 36 more hours. YIELD 1 1/2 QUARTS

raspberry vanilla-almond granola

chocolate-ginger macaroons

This is one of the easiest raw food recipes that I have ever prepared, and we have created many variations of it. The macaroons are also great with raw cacao nibs or with chopped almonds or hazelnuts.

1 3/4 cups dried coconut
3/4 cup macadamia nuts, chopped
3/4 cup + 2 tablespoons cocoa powder
3/4 cup maple syrup

1/4 cup + 2 tablespoons coconut oil
1 tablespoon ground ginger
1 1/4 teaspoons vanilla extract
Pinch sea salt

Mix together all dry ingredients. Add wet ingredients to dry mixture and mix thoroughly. Place small scoops onto Teflex sheets and press down very slightly. Dehydrate 1 day. Transfer to dehydrator screens and dehydrate 1 more day. YIELD 22–24

vanilla-almond macaroons

Something about the combination of ingredients gives these cookies a buttery flavor. I prefer them warm right out of the dehydrator.

1 3/4 cups dried coconut
3/4 cup ground almonds
3/4 cup + 2 tablespoons almond or cashew flour
3/4 cup maple syrup

1/3 cup coconut oil
1 1/4 teaspoons vanilla extract
1/2 teaspoon almond extract
Pinch sea salt

Mix together dry ingredients. Add wet ingredients to dry mixture and mix thoroughly. Place small scoops onto Teflex sheets and press down. Dehydrate 1 day. Transfer to dehydrator screens and dehydrate 1 more day. YIELD 22–24

chocolate-ginger and vanilla-almond macaroons

super goji-cacao-maca bars

These granola bars are definitely not lacking in nutrition—maca is a great source of protein and is often referred to as a natural source of testosterone. Despite the amount of agave, the bars are not that sweet, due to the density of the other ingredients. For a slightly softer and sweeter bar, just increase the agave by 20 percent.

4³/₄ cups Almond Crumbs (see recipe below)
3 cups cashew pieces
1 cup hemp seeds
¹/₂ cup golden flax seeds, soaked 2 hours and drained
1 teaspoon sea salt
1 teaspoon vanilla extract

1 teaspoon lemon zest, finely chopped
1³/₄ cups agave
¹/₄ cup maca
¹/₂ cup cacao nibs
1 cup goji berries, soaked no more than 15 minutes and drained
1 recipe Sweet Cacao Sauce (see recipe page 116)

Mix all ingredients in large bowl until incorporated. Spread evenly on a parchment-lined half sheet pan and press firmly. Dehydrate overnight. Loosen all sides of pan and turn out onto cutting board. Trim edges and cut into bars. Glaze bars with Sweet Cacao Sauce. Return to dehydrator screens and dehydrate overnight. YIELD 32 BARS

almond crumbs

Almond crumbs are a valuable ingredient when texture is needed in a recipe.

8 cups almonds

Simply place the almonds (unsoaked) in a food processor and blend until ground but still slightly coarse. YIELD 3¹/₂ CUPS

super goji-cacao-maca bars

raw chocolate chip cookies

It is sometimes best to make these in large batches. By the time they are fully dehydrated, someone may have already eaten most of them!

2^1/$_2$ cups fine cashew flour
1^3/$_4$ cups oat flour
^{1}/$_2$ cup raw cacao powder
^{1}/$_4$ cup water

^{3}/$_4$ cup maple syrup
1 tablespoon vanilla extract
1^1/$_2$ teaspoons sea salt
1 cup + a few extra Raw Chocolate Chips (see recipe below)

Mix all ingredients except chocolate chips in a medium-sized bowl by hand. Stir in 1 cup chocolate chips. Form into 3-inch cookies and press a few extra chocolate chips into the top of each cookie. Dehydrate on screens overnight at 118 degrees. YIELD 22–24

raw chocolate chips

One of the great challenges in preparing raw foods is the search to replace some very popular foods. Chocolate chips are one such example. Fortunately, a very talented chef I have worked with, Kristen Reyes, discovered this method.

1^3/$_4$ cups cashews, soaked 1–2 hours
1 cup maple syrup

1 cup raw cacao powder
^{1}/$_4$ teaspoon vanilla extract
^{1}/$_2$ teaspoon sea salt

Place all ingredients in Vita-Mix and blend until smooth. Place in piping bag and pipe chocolate chips onto Teflex sheet. Dehydrate overnight at 118 degrees. Keep in refrigerator in a sealed container until ready to use. YIELD 2 CUPS

raw chocolate chip cookies

unbaked

Crackers and breads are one of the most challenging aspects of raw food preparation. Because most traditional recipes require both flour and baking, two nonexistent components

ERS,
BREADS,

in raw, we have had to rethink everything. Slowly, over time, our kitchen has produced some very respectable variations. These all keep quite well and have multiple uses.

CHIPS

cumin flatbread

This flatbread was made by two former colleagues, Anna and Kristen, for a Mediterranean dinner we were preparing. It has an incredible similarity to the texture of its original source of inspiration. It is versatile enough to be used for anything—a sandwich, a pizza, or a snack by itself.

1 cup flax meal
1 tablespoon dried basil
2 yellow squash, roughly chopped
1 1/2 cups walnuts, soaked 6–8 hours
4 teaspoons ground cumin

1/4 cup olive oil
1 shallot, minced
1 tablespoon nutritional yeast
2 tablespoons agave
1 1/2 teaspoons sea salt
Black pepper

Place flax meal in a medium-sized bowl. Process remaining ingredients in a food processor until smooth. Add mixture to bowl with flax meal and stir until well combined. Spread on Teflex sheets to 1/3 inch thickness. You can sprinkle with a bit of extra cumin and salt, if desired. Dehydrate at 115 degrees for 6–8 hours until almost completely dry but still a bit pliable. Transfer bread to dehydrator screens and dehydrate 24 hours. YIELD ABOUT 2 DOZEN PIECES

herb crackers

This is a basic all-purpose cracker. Think of it as a raw Ritz.

4 3/4 cups almond flour
1 cup oat flour (see subrecipe page 52)
2 teaspoons sea salt + more for sprinkling
1 cup flax meal
2 tablespoons nutritional yeast

2 teaspoons well-chopped fresh oregano
4 teaspoons well-chopped fresh thyme
4 teaspoons well-chopped fresh rosemary
2 tablespoons olive oil
2 cups water

Mix all ingredients together in a large bowl. Spread very thin on Teflex sheets, about 1 cup per sheet. Cut with pizza cutter, 8 across and 8 down, to make 64 crackers per sheet. Sprinkle with sea salt. Dehydrate 2 days. Transfer to dehydrator screens and dehydrate another 12 hours, until crisp. YIELD 6 TRAYS OF 64 CRACKERS

golden tortilla chips

Frozen corn works better in this recipe—it is one of those raw food mysteries that we can't fully explain.

1³/4 cups flax meal
4 cups frozen corn, thawed
1¹/3 cups water
2¹/2 tablespoons olive oil
1 tablespoon cumin
³/4 small red onion

1 clove garlic
¹/4 tablespoon sea salt + more for sprinkling
1 tablespoon + 1 teaspoon lime juice
Pinch cayenne
2 teaspoons chili powder

Place flax meal in a large bowl. Blend all remaining ingredients except chili powder in a Vita-Mix or high-speed blender until smooth. Stir in flax meal and chili powder. Spread one cup of batter over the entire Teflex sheet to no more than 1/8 inch thickness and place in dehydrator. Approximately 30 minutes later the chips will be ready to be removed and marked with a paring knife into the size and shape you desire. Sprinkle with salt and dehydrate 12–24 hours, until completely crispy. YIELD 4 TRAYS

za'atar flatbread

Za'atar is a lemony spice mix most commonly used in Lebanon. I was introduced to it by a Lebanese friend years ago and have always loved it on a plain pizza or flatbread. These za'atar crackers are quite good on their own.

6 whole roma tomatoes, chopped
³/4 teaspoon garam masala
2 tablespoons za'atar spice mix, divided in half
1 tablespoon cumin
¹/2 teaspoon sea salt, or to taste*

¹/2 cup flax meal
¹/2 cup sesame seeds
1 cup sunflower seeds, soaked 4–5 hours
1 cup flax seeds, soaked 15–20 minutes

Blend roma tomatoes, garam masala, 1 tablespoon za'atar spice mix, cumin, and salt in Vita-Mix; set aside. In a large bowl, mix flax meal, sesame seeds, sunflower seeds, and flax seeds. Add tomato mixture to bowl and mix until dough-like texture is achieved. Spread thin layer over Teflex sheet with an off-set spatula, about 1-1/4 cups per sheet. Precut crackers with knife or pizza cutter to desired size. Sprinkle each sheet with a little of the remaining 1 tablespoon za'atar spice mix. Dehydrate at 118 degrees for 24–36 hours, until crackers are fully dry. YIELD 2 TRAYS OF 22 CRACKERS

*Use caution when salting raw foods! Foods become saltier after dehydration.

bar-b-que crisps

Growing up, I loved barbecued potato chips, but not how they made me feel. This is the closest I've tasted in the raw world.

BAR-B-QUE SAUCE
1 3/4 cups sun-dried tomatoes, soaked 3 hours,
   drained, and chopped (reserve soaking water)
1/2 cup sun-dried tomato soaking water
1/3 cup maple syrup
1/4 cup + 3 tablespoons apple cider vinegar
2 small shallots, peeled and chopped
2 small cloves garlic, peeled
1/4 cup chipotle chiles, soaked 2 hours
   (reserve soaking water)
1/4 cup chipotle chile soaking water
4 teaspoons chili powder
1 teaspoon nama shoyu

BAR-B-QUE SPICE MIX
1 tablespoon sea salt
2 tablespoons maple syrup
2 tablespoons chili powder
2 teaspoons sumac

OAT FLOUR
8 quarts oat groats

BAR-B-QUE CHIPS
4 cups almond flour
1 cup oat flour
2 teaspoons sea salt
1 cup flax meal
2 tablespoons nutritional yeast
2 tablespoons olive oil
2 cups Bar-B-Que Sauce
1 recipe Bar-B-Que Spice Mix

BAR-B-QUE SAUCE
Blend all ingredients in Vita-Mix. Store in refrigerator.

BAR-B-QUE SPICE MIX
Mix ingredients together in a small bowl.

OAT FLOUR
Blend 2 cups of oats at a time in Vita-Mix. Make sure flour is fine, with no hard bits. Store in refrigerator.

BAR-B-QUE CHIPS
Mix all ingredients for Bar-B-Que Chips in a large bowl. Spread very thin on Teflex sheets, about 1 cup per sheet. Brush dough generously with Bar-B-Que Sauce.

Cut with pizza cutter, 8 across and 8 down, to make 64 crackers per sheet. Sprinkle generously with Bar-B-Que Spice Mix. Dehydrate 2–3 days, until crisp. **YIELD 6 TRAYS**

bar-b-que crisps, za'atar flatbread, herb crackers

starters

Raw food recipes are so unique, they are often more fun to eat tapas style—in small portions and with a large variety of dishes. I generally prefer starters anyway, and my involvement with raw cuisine has only enhanced that. Remember that smaller dishes have less time to make an impression, so seasoning is very important. For that reason, many of these recipes have extra spicy or pungent flavors that go a long way.

blueberry pancakes

Kristen Reyes, a chef who worked with me for some time, developed this recipe for a breakfast food preparation class one Saturday. I was skeptical, knowing that breads and baked items are hard to replicate in the raw kitchen. But she surprised me with this dish, which both looks and tastes like a great pancake.

3/4 cup fresh blueberries
2 ripe bananas
2 cups pecans, soaked 8–12 hours
2 cups pine nuts

1 cup water
1/2 cup agave
1 vanilla bean, scraped
1 teaspoon sea salt
2 cups maple syrup

Place blueberries in a medium bowl; set aside. Blend remaining ingredients in Vita-Mix until completely smooth. Add batter to bowl with blueberries and stir to combine. Spread batter into 4- or 5-inch rounds on dehydrator Teflex sheets. Pancakes should not be more than 1/2-inch tall. Dehydrate 24–48 hours. Serve warm with maple syrup and Eggplant Bacon (see recipe page 58). YIELD 10

> Like any other nuts and seeds, pine nuts should be stored in airtight containers in the refrigerator. Nuts can actually go bad if exposed to too much light.

blueberry pancakes

eggplant bacon

I can't claim to understand how Kristen came up with this brilliant garnish, but it's incredibly complex, interesting, and actually delicious. It keeps well, so feel free to make it a day or two ahead and use it with any breakfast-type item or even to make your own version of a raw Cobb salad.

1 large eggplant, thinly sliced lengthwise
1 tablespoon sea salt
1/2 dried chipotle chile, soaked at least 2 hours
1/2 cup soaking water from chipotle chile
2 tablespoons maple syrup
2 tablespoons olive oil

2 tablespoons nama shoyu
2 tablespoons apple cider vinegar
1 teaspoon chili powder
1/2 teaspoon paprika
1/2 teaspoon cumin
Pinch black pepper
Pinch cayenne

Toss eggplant and sea salt in a large bowl and let sit 1–2 hours. Blend remaining ingredients in Vita-Mix and place in a medium bowl. Squeeze liquid from eggplant and add slices to bowl with marinade.

Allow eggplant to marinate 30–45 minutes. Spread slices on dehydrator screens. Dehydrate 24–36 hours, until crisp, and cut into desired sizes.
YIELD 15–20

Maple syrup is not raw. The sap is gathered from the maple tree and is actually boiled for refinement, resulting in a thick syrup. Use sparingly as its distinctive flavor can overwhelm other ingredients.

cucumber–white grape gazpacho

I have loved gazpacho since my first visit to Spain. I actually prefer a lighter white gazpacho like this to the more popular red tomato–based ones.

2 cups peeled, seeded, and diced cucumbers
2 cups seeded and diced tomatillos

2 cups diced white grapes
$1/4$ cup ginger juice
Salt and freshly ground white pepper to taste

Mix all ingredients in a large bowl; season to taste. Place three-fourths of the mixture in a food processor and process until smooth. Add back to bowl with remaining fruit and vegetables and stir to combine. Serve chilled. SERVES 2

portobello sausage

Portobello mushrooms are very meaty and are probably the best type of mushroom for this dish, but it would also work with a cremini or even a white button mushroom.

3 tablespoons olive oil
2 tablespoons nama shoyu
1 tablespoon umeboshi plum paste
1 tablespoon apple cider vinegar
4 cups chopped portobello mushrooms
2 cups chopped eggplant
1 cup almonds, soaked 8–12 hours

1 cup pumpkin seeds, soaked 8–12 hours
1 tablespoon coriander
4 scallions, chopped
1 clove garlic, minced
1 cup parsley, coarsely chopped
Sea salt to taste
Black pepper to taste

In a large bowl, whisk together olive oil, nama shoyu, plum paste, and apple cider vinegar. Toss in mushrooms and eggplant, and allow to marinate 15–20 minutes.

Process almonds, pumpkin seeds, and coriander in food processor into small pieces; do not overprocess. Place mixture in large bowl. Process marinated mushrooms and eggplant with scallions, garlic, and parsley in food processor until chunky; add to bowl with almonds and pumpkin seeds.

Stir mixture until ingredients are well combined and season with salt and pepper. Shape mixture in patties or balls and place on dehydrator screens. Dehydrate 8–12 hours, until crust forms on outside.
YIELD 15–20

portobello sausage

tofu scrambler

This is a very ingenious recipe that was developed at The Plant Restaurant when it was open in Brooklyn. It is highly satisfying and quite easy to prepare as well.

2 teaspoons nutritional yeast
$1/4$ teaspoon turmeric
Black pepper to taste

1 teaspoon nama shoyu
1 recipe Silken Tofu (see recipe page 66)

Add nutritional yeast, turmeric, black pepper, and nama shoyu to tofu. Mash well with fork until all ingredients are combined. Keep cool until ready to serve. SERVES 2

tofu scrambler

sesame cashew dumplings

These tasty dumplings are so popular and are great for parties or guests who have never had raw food. The coconut wrappers are one of the best inventions I have found in experimenting with raw food.

COCONUT WRAPPERS (MAKES 3–4 SHEETS)
4 cups young coconut meat, chopped
$1/2$ teaspoon sea salt
$1/4$ cup carrot, beet, or spinach juice

CASHEW FILLING (MAKES 4 CUPS)
4 cups cashews, soaked 1–2 hours
6 tablespoons nama shoyu
6 tablespoons sesame oil
$1/4$ cup raw tahini
2 tablespoons finely chopped fresh ginger

1 quart carrots, finely diced in food processor
1 quart celery, finely diced in food processor
$1/2$ cup minced scallions
Sea salt and pepper to taste

MARINATED SPINACH
4 cups spinach, torn by hand
2 tablespoons sesame oil
1 tablespoon finely chopped fresh ginger
$1/2$ teaspoon sea salt
1 teaspoon chili powder

COCONUT WRAPPERS

Blend coconut meat and salt in Vita-Mix until very smooth. Add vegetable juice to color the wrappers as desired, or divide the mixture into 3 smaller batches and prepare different colors by using different juices. Spread mixture in a thin, even layer over a Teflex sheet and dehydrate for 4–5 hours. Trim the outer edges of each sheet by about 1/4–1/2 inch; cut each sheet into 9 even squares. Wrap in plastic and store in refrigerator. Remove wrappers from refrigerator and bring to room temperature prior to use.

CASHEW FILLING

Process cashews, nama shoyu, sesame oil, tahini, and ginger in food processor until chunky consistency is achieved. Mix carrots, celery, and scallions with cashew nut meat together in a large bowl and adjust seasoning to taste.

MARINATED SPINACH

Toss spinach with the sesame oil, ginger, salt, and chili powder. Let sit 10–15 minutes at room temperature to wilt.

ASSEMBLY

Lay Coconut Wrappers out on a cool workspace. Dab very lightly with water. Place a small amount of Marinated Spinach on each. Top with 1 tablespoon of the Cashew Filling. Pull edges up around filling to form a half-circle dumpling. Serve with Sweet Chili–Lime Sauce (see recipe page 73).
YIELD APPROXIMATELY 2 DOZEN DUMPLINGS

sesame cashew dumplings

miso soup

This soup is actually great served cold; but if you prefer it slightly warmer, simply place in the dehydrator for about 30 minutes before serving.

3 cups water
$^1/_4$ cup nama shoyu
$^1/_4$ cup sesame oil
$^1/_4$ cup dried dulse

$^1/_2$ cup mellow white miso
1 recipe Silken Tofu (see recipe below)
$^1/_4$ cup enoki mushrooms, for garnish
2 tablespoons diagonally sliced scallions, for garnish

Blend water, nama shoyu, sesame oil, dulse, and miso in blender until smooth. Pour broth into bowls and place 4 cubes of tofu in each bowl. To garnish, divide the enoki mushrooms and scallions among the bowls. SERVES 2

Raw carrageenan is prepared by washing salt-packed Irish moss in cold water until all salt is removed. The Irish moss is soaked overnight, and then blended with an equal amount of water until smooth. You can store it in the refrigerator for up to 1 week.

silken tofu

The day I first tasted this, I was thrilled to discover that a raw version of tofu could be so light. While many find tofu bland, I have always loved its versatility and even taste.

1 cup cashews, soaked 1–2 hours
$^1/_2$ cup fresh young Thai coconut meat

$^1/_2$ cup raw carrageenan
$^1/_4$ cup water
$^1/_4$ teaspoon sea salt

Line the bottom and sides of a small pan or square container with plastic wrap. Drain cashews. Blend all ingredients in Vita-Mix until completely smooth. Pour into lined pan and cover with plastic wrap. Tofu should be about 1 1/2 inches thick. Refrigerate about 2 hours until firm. When ready to serve, remove tofu from container by lifting plastic wrap out of pan and gently transferring tofu to a cutting board. Cut into 2-inch squares with a butter knife. YIELD 8–10 PIECES

miso soup and silken tofu

marinated kalamata olives

Perfect as a starter to any dinner, this recipe is simple to make and is great when served with hummus, tabbouleh, and flax crackers.

3 cups kalamata olives
1/2 teaspoon ground coriander seed
1/4 cup chopped mint leaves

1/4 cup chopped parsley
1/4 cup olive oil
1 tablespoon orange zest

If using whole kalamata olives, be sure to remove pits prior to using. Transfer olives to medium bowl, add rest of ingredients, toss, and season to taste. Allow to marinate 1–2 hours. YIELD 2–3 CUPS

savory crepes

The use of squash and zucchini in dehydrated recipes creates a very soft, pliable texture, which is perfect for something like crepes. These are very filling and make a great brunch dish.

CREPES
1/2 cup flax meal
1/2 cup chopped yellow squash
1/4 cup chopped young coconut meat
1 1/2 teaspoons lemon juice
1 cup water
1 tablespoon agave
1/4 teaspoon sea salt
1/4 teaspoon coriander
1/4 teaspoon cumin

ASSEMBLY
2 cups spinach, torn by hand

1 1/2 teaspoon olive oil
1/2 teaspoon sea salt
1 cup seeded and chopped tomatoes
   or 1 cup halved cherry tomatoes
1 cup chopped portobello mushroom caps
1/2 cup sliced red onion
2 tablespoons nama shoyu
2 tablespoons olive oil
1 tablespoon apple cider vinegar
4 crepes
Portobello Sausage (see recipe page 60)
Lemon-Thyme Yogurt Sauce (see recipe page 77)

CREPES
Blend all ingredients in Vita-Mix until smooth. Spread thinly into 6- to 7-inch rounds on Teflex dehydrator sheets. Dehydrate 5–6 hours until dry but very pliable.

ASSEMBLY
Toss spinach with 1-1/2 teaspoon olive oil and salt; let sit in warm area for 15–20 minutes. Toss vegetables with nama shoyu, 2 tablespoons olive oil, and apple cider vinegar; let sit 20–30 minutes. Spread vegetables on Teflex dehydrator sheets and dehydrate at 115 degrees for 30 minutes, until veggies are soft and well marinated.

Combine spinach and marinated veggies in a medium bowl, cover with plastic wrap, and refrigerate or keep warm in dehydrator until ready to serve.

Fill each crepe with 1/2 cup vegetable mixture plus Portobello Sausage pieces. Fold into desired shape. Drizzle Lemon-Thyme Yogurt Sauce over crepes and serve. YIELD 8–10

marinated kalamata olives

spreads, dips & sauces

CIOUS and

For someone like me, who likes the spirit of tapas and enjoys small tastes, these spreads, dips, and sauces are always welcome. Most can be made ahead and keep quite well. I love having them to enjoy with crackers or simply raw vegetables for elevated crudités.

TASTES

chipotle mayo

This dressing has many uses—due to its texture and weight, it is best as a condiment with firm vegetables such as jicama, but also is great spread on a cracker or sprouted bread.

1 cup macadamia nuts, soaked 1–2 hours
1 chipotle chile, soaked 1–2 hours

1 cup soaking water from chile
1 1/2 cups olive oil
Sea salt to taste

Blend all ingredients in Vita-Mix until completely smooth. YIELD 3 CUPS

red chile–pineapple dipping sauce

I have always loved the combination of fruit and chile—this dipping sauce is good with any vegetable or lettuce wrap, or with any variation of raw dumplings.

4 cups fresh pineapple juice
1/2 cup agave

2 tablespoons red pepper flakes
2 tablespoons paprika
Sea salt to taste

Combine all ingredients in a bowl and whisk. Place bowl in dehydrator to reduce overnight. Store in refrigerator. YIELD 3 CUPS

sweet chile–lime sauce

Quick and easy sauces are a major part of making simple raw food interesting and unique. This example is not only easy but also very tasty.

3/4 cup nama shoyu
2 tablespoons agave
2 tablespoons lime juice

1 tablespoon sesame oil
Pinch red pepper flakes

Combine all ingredients in a bowl and whisk until well blended. YIELD 1 CUP

macadamia hummus

When I first began experimenting with raw food, I read that chickpeas were good sprouted and then used to prepare hummus. I actually found sprouted chickpea hummus to be grainy and heavy, and one day experimented with cashews with success. This version uses macadamia nuts, which are my personal favorite.

3 cups macadamia nuts, soaked 1–2 hours
1/4 cup lemon juice
3 tablespoons olive oil
1/2 cup raw tahini

1 teaspoon sea salt
1 1/4 cups water
1 small clove garlic

Blend all ingredients in Vita-Mix until smooth and creamy. Add water if necessary to obtain a looser consistency. YIELD 1 QUART

salsa fresca

This is best if it sits for a couple of hours; but once you add the salt, it should be no more than 4 hours, as it may become watery.

4 cups seeded and diced tomatoes
1 cup minced red onion

1 cup chopped fresh cilantro
1/4 cup lime juice
2 teaspoons sea salt

Mix all ingredients in a large bowl. YIELD 1 1/2 QUARTS

mango guacamole

I have never met someone who didn't love guacamole. I personally love it—there is a Mexican restaurant in Manhattan's East Village that I go to specifically for their many variations.

7 avocados
2 teaspoons sea salt
2 cups chopped cilantro

3 seeded jalapeños, chopped
2 tablespoons lime juice
2 mangoes, finely chopped

Place all ingredients except mango in food processor. Pulse until well combined but not too smooth. Remove to a bowl and stir in the mango. Cover with plastic wrap pressed against the surface of the guacamole to prevent oxidizing. Store in refrigerator. YIELD 1 QUART

macadamia feta cheese

Sprinkle this on salads or even a zucchini pasta with olives and tomatoes.

2 cups macadamia nuts, soaked 1–2 hours
2 tablespoons lemon juice
1 tablespoon nutritional yeast

$1/2$ medium shallot
$3/4$ teaspoon sea salt

Process all ingredients in food processor until well combined. Crumble cheese onto dehydrator screens and dehydrate for 4–6 hours. Store in refrigerator.
YIELD 2 CUPS

> The monosaturated oil of macadamia nuts is not only good for the heart, but a very effective metabolism booster as well.

macadamia red pepper cheese

This is a great spread to use on a cracker or to make a Middle Eastern–style pizza with vegetables.

2 cups macadamia nuts, soaked 2 hours
3 tablespoons nutritional yeast
$1^{1}/2$ teaspoons sea salt
Pinch cayenne pepper

$1/2$ tablespoon lemon zest
$1/2$ cup water
$1/2$ cup chopped red bell pepper
$1/2$ shallot, peeled
$1/4$ clove garlic

Mix together nuts, yeast, salt, and cayenne. Add lemon zest, water, bell pepper, shallot, and garlic and mix thoroughly. Place small scoops onto Teflex sheets and press down very slightly. Dehydrate 1 day. Transfer to dehydrator screens and dehydrate 1 more day. YIELD 22–24 SERVINGS

pineapple mango salsa

This is a great all-purpose sauce, which goes really well with nearly any vegetable preparation.

2 cups finely diced pineapple
2 cups finely diced mango
1 cup finely diced red bell pepper

1/4 cup minced jalapeño
1/4 cup chopped cilantro
1/4 cup lime juice
Sea salt to taste

Gently mix all ingredients in a bowl. YIELD 1 QUART

black olive pesto

This recipe really is a combination of a pesto and a tapenade. It's great on flatbreads and crackers, or used as a dipping sauce.

1 cup sun-dried tomatoes, soaked 1–2 hours and drained
1 cup pine nuts
2 cups kalamata olives, pitted

2 cups fresh basil leaves, packed
1 cup fresh parsley
1/4 cup olive oil

Combine sun-dried tomatoes, pine nuts, and olives in a food processor; pulse until chunky. Pour into medium bowl and set aside. Add basil, parsley, and olive oil to food processor; pulse to form a chunky pesto. Add basil mixture to bowl with sun-dried tomato mixture and mix well. YIELD 2 CUPS

lemon-thyme yogurt sauce

Cashews and coconuts are the building blocks for many of our creams, sauces, and desserts. There is almost no coconut flavor in this dish, which has a texture like the full-bodied Greek yogurts.

1 3/4 cups cashews, soaked 1–2 hours
1/2 cup young coconut meat
1/4 cup water

6 tablespoons lemon juice
Zest of 2 lemons
2 tablespoons finely minced fresh thyme

Blend all ingredients except thyme in Vita-Mix until smooth and creamy. Add thyme and blend for a few moments until thyme is well incorporated. Serve or store in refrigerator 3–4 days. YIELD 3 CUPS

roasted pepper hummus with lime

Due to their water content, red bell peppers become very intense in flavor when dehydrated. They add a lot to this straightforward hummus recipe, which is great on its own or as a component of a more complex recipe.

2 cups seeded and chopped red bell peppers
2 cups cashews, soaked 1–2 hours
1 cup macadamia nuts, soaked 1–2 hours
1/2 cup lime juice

3 tablespoons olive oil
1/2 cup raw tahini
1 teaspoon sea salt
1 1/4 cups water

Place red bell peppers on dehydrator screen and dehydrate at 118 degrees for 24 hours. Blend all ingredients in Vita-Mix until smooth and creamy. Add more water if necessary to obtain a looser consistency. YIELD 1 QUART

chili

Often, a raw food dish is a result of choosing a great ingredient and preparing it simply—other times, getting a recipe right can require exhaustive experimentation. It took a lot to get this right, but it was well worth the effort.

1 portobello mushroom, finely chopped
$1/2$ cup minced celery
$1/2$ cup chopped red onion
1 red bell pepper, finely chopped
1 cup almonds, soaked 4–6 hours
1 cup chopped carrots
$1 1/2$ cups sun-dried tomatoes, soaked
2 cups water, fresh or from sun-dried tomatoes
　　soaking liquid

1 tablespoon olive oil
$1/4$ cup nama shoyu
1 clove garlic
2 tablespoons fresh oregano
1 tablespoon dry oregano
2 teaspoons chili powder
1 tablespoon cumin
1 tablespoon apple cider vinegar
1 tablespoon agave
$1/4$ teaspoon cayenne pepper

Place mushrooms, celery, onion, and bell pepper in a large bowl. Pulse almonds and carrots in food processor until a chunky consistency is achieved; add to bowl. Blend remaining ingredients in Vita-Mix until smooth; add to bowl and mix all ingredients until well combined. Store in refrigerator and warm in dehydrator prior to serving. YIELD 2 QUARTS

sour cream

This is good on anything, especially chili (see recipe above) and mango guacamole (see recipe page 74).

2 cups cashews, soaked 4–6 hours
1 cup water

$1/2$ cup olive oil
3 tablespoons lemon juice
$1 1/2$ teaspoons salt

Blend all ingredients in Vita-Mix until completely smooth. YIELD 1 QUART

chili, sour cream, salsa fresca, and mango guacamole

salads

If I could take one food to a deserted island, and it wasn't chocolate, it would be a salad. I have always loved them and now, I occasionally live on them. There are no limitations in terms of what can be added; they

YOUR everyday SALADS

are the easiest and fastest way to put many elements together and are loaded with nutrition. I prefer mine large, and not too late in the day, as they need to be eaten slowly and given plenty of time to digest.

blue green salad

This signature salad, named after one of my earlier juice bars, combines many of my favorite ingredients into one dish; it makes a great light lunch.

2 handfuls mixed greens
1 sliced tomato
$1/2$ cup dried dulse, torn into 1-inch pieces
1 cup finely diced cucumber
1 whole avocado, sliced

Sea salt to taste
Freshly ground black pepper to taste
$1/4$ cup Spicy Almond Dressing (see recipe below)
$1/2$ cup sunflower, buckwheat, or other sprouts
$1/2$ cup hemp seeds

Place a handful of mixed greens in the center of each plate. Top with tomato, dulse, cucumber, and avocado. Season with salt and pepper.

Drizzle generously with dressing just before serving or place dressing in a small bowl on plate next to salad. Garnish with sprouts and hemp seeds. SERVES 2

spicy almond dressing

2 cups almond butter
4 roma tomatoes
$1/2$ cup nama shoyu
$1/4$ cup sesame oil
3 tablespoons lime juice

2 teaspoons maple syrup
1 teaspoon miso
3-inch piece ginger
1-inch piece lemon grass
6–8 Thai chiles
1 teaspoon sea salt

Blend all ingredients in Vita-Mix until completely smooth. Thin with water as needed. YIELD 1 QUART

seaweed salad

Sea vegetables are one of the most nutritious foods we can eat, and, fortunately, they are also delicious. With varying textures, colors, and flavors, their briny ocean taste works well with pungent fruits, creamy dressings, and spicy flavors like ginger. The green mango in this recipe provides a much-needed textural contrast that also rounds out the Asian influence of the dish.

2 cups mixed greens
1/2 cup dried wakame in 1-inch pieces, soaked 20–30 minutes and drained
1/2 cup dried arame in 1-inch pieces, soaked 5–10 minutes and drained
1/2 cup dried hijiki in 1-inch pieces, soaked 20–30 minutes and drained
1/2 cup julienned green mango

1/2 cup julienned cucumber
1/2 cup julienned beets
Sea salt
1/4 cup dressing
  Ginger-Miso Dressing (see recipe below),
  Creamy Sesame Dressing (see recipe page 84), or
  Sweet Miso Dressing (see recipe page 88)
2 tablespoons white sesame seeds
2 tablespoons finely chopped scallions

Place 1 cup of mixed greens in the center of each plate. Mix all the seaweeds in a medium bowl. Add all the julienned vegetables. Salt to taste. Place equal amounts of the sea vegetable mixture on top of the greens.

Just before serving, drizzle generously with dressing and sprinkle with sesame seeds and scallions.
SERVES 2

ginger-miso dressing

1/2 cup white miso
1/3 cup agave
1/3 cup apple cider vinegar

1/4 cup sesame oil
1/4 cup lemon juice
1 1/4 cups chopped fresh ginger

Blend all ingredients in Vita-Mix until completely smooth. YIELD 1 QUART

potato salad

This dish reminds me of a South American version of potato salad we had growing up in Maine, but it is more sophisticated and far lighter.

2 cups diced jicama
1/4 cup diced yellow pepper
1/4 cup diced celery
1 tablespoon minced fresh rosemary

2 tablespoons minced green olives
1/4 avocado, mashed
1/2 red onion, thinly sliced
Fresh parsley sprigs, for garnish

In a bowl, combine all ingredients except parsley sprigs and set aside. If not using right away, put in a container and store in refrigerator. When ready to serve, pour Potato Salad Dressing (see recipe below) over salad and toss until well combined. Divide salad between two serving plates and garnish with parsley sprigs. SERVES 2

potato salad dressing

2 tablespoons tahini
1/4 teaspoon ground cumin
1 1/2 tablespoons lemon juice
2 tablespoons water

2 teaspoons fresh parsley
1/4 teaspoon nama shoyu
1/4 teaspoon agave
Pinch sea salt
Pinch chili powder

Blend all ingredients in a Vita-Mix or blender until smooth. Dressing should be thick, as it will thin out when stirred with jicama. SERVES 2

creamy sesame dressing

This dressing is particularly good with seaweed; it's also very well matched for sturdy greens or even chopped vegetables.

1/2 cup nama shoyu
1/2 cup tahini
1/4 cup sesame oil
2 tablespoons agave

1/4 cup apple cider vinegar
1 teaspoon sea salt
1-inch piece ginger
1/4 cup olive oil
1 teaspoon lime juice

Blend all ingredients in blender until smooth.

YIELD 2 CUPS

potato salad

thai salad

In the raw food world, a salad is often actually a meal, so it is quite common to go well beyond the typical definition of salad and include much sturdier ingredients in a wide variety.

2 handfuls mixed greens
1/2 cup finely diced pineapple
1/2 cup soaked, finely sliced sun-dried tomatoes
1 avocado, sliced
Sea salt

Freshly ground black pepper
1/2 red bell pepper, cut into long, thin strips
1/2 cup thinly sliced young coconut meat
1/2 cup chopped Curried Cashews (see recipe page 39)
1/2 cup Creamy Thai Dressing (see recipe below)
Cilantro leaves, for garnish

Place a handful of mixed greens in the center of each plate. Top with pineapple, sun-dried tomatoes, and avocado. Season with salt and pepper to taste.

Top with red bell pepper, coconut, and Curried Cashews. Drizzle dressing generously over top just before serving. Garnish with cilantro leaves. SERVES 2

creamy thai dressing

I recently had this dressing on a sea vegetable salad; it is really spicy, so be careful.

3/4 cup sesame oil
1/2 cup nama shoyu
1/4 cup olive oil
1/4 cup lime juice

1 tablespoon maple syrup
4 Thai bird chiles or 3 teaspoons red chili flakes
1 teaspoon sea salt
1/4 cup chopped cashews

Blend all ingredients in a blender until smooth.
YIELD 2 1/2 CUPS

thai salad

tabbouleh

I rarely advocate the use of sprouted grains, although they are technically raw. I find them hard to digest and not that pleasant to eat. Quinoa, however, becomes quite good when sprouted, and I love its nutty flavor and the fact that it is an excellent source of protein.

1 cup quinoa, rinsed and soaked for 24 hours
1/4 cup olive oil
3 tablespoons lemon juice
1 teaspoon sea salt

1 cup seeded and diced cucumber
1 cup seeded and diced roma tomato
1/4 cup minced red onion
1/2 cup flat Italian parsley

Drain quinoa; transfer to a medium bowl and marinate in olive oil, lemon juice, and salt for 30 minutes to 1 hour. Add remaining ingredients and toss until well incorporated.

Eat immediately or let flavors marinate for an hour prior to serving. SERVES 2

sweet miso dressing

This is as much of a dipping sauce as a dressing—it is multidimensional, really, and goes well with any salad, sea vegetable, or roll.

1/4 cup tahini
1/4 cup agave

1 tablespoon water
2 tablespoons mellow white miso
1 1/2 teaspoons fresh lemon juice

Prepare dressing by placing all ingredients in a small bowl and whisking until very well combined.

Or place in a blender and blend until smooth.
YIELD 2 CUPS

blood orange–crispy fennel salad

Fennel and orange are a classic combination. In a very direct, simple way, there is a symphony of taste, texture, and color. I first had this dish at a Tuscan restaurant many years ago and have since found it to be one of my favorite classical recipes. Little did I know at the time, I was eating raw vegan food.

2 fennel bulbs, thinly sliced (use a mandolin)
Sea salt
Black pepper
Olive oil
2 blood oranges, segmented
2 handfuls baby arugula

4 cremini mushrooms, thinly sliced
1/4 cup Macadamia Feta Cheese (see recipe page 75)
Fennel fronds, for garnish
Blood Orange Dressing (see recipe below)
Coarse sea salt, for garnish
Black sesame seeds, for garnish

Toss fennel with salt, pepper, and enough olive oil to coat. Place in dehydrator at 118 degrees until crispy. To segment a blood orange, first cut off the top and the bottom and discard; place orange on a cutting board. Remove the peel, cutting down from top to bottom, to expose the flesh. Place the blood orange directly over a bowl, and, using a paring knife, cut along each side of the membranes to separate the segments and place them in the bowl. After remov-ing all segments, squeeze out the remaining juice in a separate bowl and set it aside for the dressing.

Place equal amounts of baby arugula in the center of each plate. Top with blood oranges, sliced mush-rooms, and crispy fennel. Sprinkle with Macadamia Feta Cheese. Garnish with fennel fronds. Drizzle with Blood Orange Dressing just before serving and sprinkle with coarse sea salt and black sesame seeds for garnish. SERVES 2

blood orange dressing

3 tablespoons olive oil
1 1/2 teaspoons lime juice
1 1/2 teaspoons blood orange juice

Pinch sea salt
Freshly ground black pepper

In a nonmetallic bowl, whisk olive oil with lime and blood orange juice. Add salt and pepper to taste. SERVES 2

larger dishes

Vegetarian food is, to me, the most flavorful of all, but it can be challenging to provide the same diversity that other dishes may have. A chicken dish, for example, may have a side vegetable, starch, and a sauce, whereas many vegetarian dishes are one-dimensional. I try to avoid that in my recipes by incorporating many textural contrasts into main dishes.

tomato, basil, and ricotta pizza

My first job as a cook began in the month of July, at a Southern Italian restaurant. Tomato, basil, and ricotta were omnipresent—that experience was very positive, and I am forever attracted to all the flavors that I associate with my time there.

HERB CRUST
$1/2$ cup + $2^1/2$ tablespoons flax meal
1 tablespoon + 1 teaspoon dried basil
1 teaspoon dried oregano
$2^1/3$ cups roughly chopped yellow squash
1 cup walnuts, soaked 8–10 hours
2 teaspoons sea salt
$2^1/2$ tablespoons olive oil
$1/3$ shallot, minced
2 teaspoons nutritional yeast
2 teaspoons agave
2 teaspoons lemon juice
Pinch black pepper

SAUCE
$1^1/3$ cups seeded and chopped tomatoes
$1^1/3$ cups sun-dried tomatoes, soaked 15–20 minutes
$1/3$ cup soaking liquid from sun-dried tomatoes
$1/3$ teaspoon sea salt
Black pepper
$1/4$ teaspoon dried oregano

$1/4$ teaspoon dried basil
1 tablespoon + 1 teaspoon fresh oregano
1 teaspoon agave

MACADAMIA MOZZARELLA
1 cup macadamia nuts, soaked 2 hours
$3/4$ teaspoon lemon zest
$1/4$ cup water
$1/4$ shallot, peeled
$1/4$ clove garlic
$1/2$ cup nutritional yeast
$1/2$ teaspoon sea salt
Pinch cayenne

ASSEMBLY
$2^1/2$ cups packed fresh spinach or arugula
Olive oil
Sea salt
Black pepper
4 tomatoes, quartered and sliced
Basil leaves, for garnish

HERB CRUST
Place flax meal, basil, and oregano in a medium bowl; set aside. Put remaining ingredients in a food processor and process until smooth. Add processed ingredients to bowl with flax meal and stir until well combined. Spread on Teflex sheet in desired shape to 1/2 inch thickness. Dehydrate at 115 degrees for 24–36 hours, until almost completely dry but still a bit pliable. The crust will shrink a lot while dehydrating.

SAUCE
Blend all ingredients in Vita-Mix or food processor until smooth.

MACADAMIA MOZZARELLA
Blend ingredients in Vita-Mix until smooth and creamy.

ASSEMBLY
In a large bowl, toss spinach or arugula with enough olive oil to cover, and salt and pepper. In another bowl, toss tomatoes with enough olive oil to cover, and salt and pepper. Spread tomato slices on Teflex dehydrator sheets; dehydrate 1–2 hours at 115 degrees. Remove and allow to cool.

To assemble the pizza, spread the sauce on the Herb Crust, top with Macadamia Mozzarella, then marinated spinach or arugula, and dehydrated tomato slices. Garnish with fresh basil leaves. YIELD 1 PIZZA

tomato, basil, and ricotta pizza

mango wraps

One of the chefs I worked with, Loren Bruni, created this colorful dish. It is very light and refreshing, and, given its apparent complexity, is quite easy to prepare.

MANGO WRAPPERS
4 cups chopped fresh mango
2 cups fresh young coconut meat
Pinch cayenne
Pinch sea salt
1/4 cup cilantro, roughly chopped

ASSEMBLY
4 Mango Wrappers
4 romaine lettuce leaves
1 cup julienned young coconut meat
1 cup julienned carrots
1 cup julienned red bell pepper
1/4 cup fresh mint, roughly chopped
1/4 cup cilantro, roughly chopped
1/2 cup Creamy Thai Dressing (see recipe page 86)

MANGO WRAPPERS
Place all ingredients except cilantro in large container. Blend well until smooth. Spread mixture thinly on Teflex sheets and sprinkle with cilantro. Dehydrate 4 hours, until dry but still very pliable. Cut each sheet into 4 squares.

ASSEMBLY
Place 4 Mango Wrappers on a work surface, shiny side up. Place romaine leaves in center of each wrapper and top with equal portions of coconut, carrots, bell pepper, mint, and cilantro, in that order. Roll tightly and secure with a bit of water. Serve with Creamy Thai Dressing for dipping. SERVES 2

> If you ever see Thai mangoes in the market, scoop them up. They are flatter than common mangoes with a yellow skin and somewhat stringy flesh. Their flavor is even more exotic and intoxicating than regular mangoes.

portobello fajitas

Portobello mushrooms are one of those ingredients that everyone seems to love these days, including me. If you have the components of this dish prepared ahead, it is very easy to put together for guests.

TORTILLAS
1 recipe Golden Tortilla Chips batter (see recipe page 51)

SPINACH AND RED PEPPER MIX
3 portobello mushroom caps, cut into 1/2-inch slices
1/2 cup olive oil, divided
1 1/4 teaspoons sea salt
2 red bell peppers, julienned
1 small red onion, sliced

2 cups baby spinach
1 clove garlic, chopped

ASSEMBLY
2 Tortillas
1/2 cup Spinach and Red Pepper Mix
1/4 cup Sour Cream (see recipe page 78)
1/4 cup Salsa Fresca (see recipe page 74)
1/4 avocado, peeled and sliced

TORTILLAS
Spread 1/4 cup of batter in a 6" circle (per tortilla) on Teflex sheet.

Dehydrate approximately 4 hours, until it is easy to flip tortilla over. Once flipped over, continue to dehydrate until all wet spots have disappeared but tortilla is still soft and pliable, which could be 30–60 minutes longer.

Extra tortillas can be covered with plastic wrap and stored in the refrigerator for almost one week.

SPINACH AND RED PEPPER MIX
Toss mushroom slices in 1/4 cup olive oil and sea salt; spread slices on Teflex sheets and dehydrate 1–2 hours, until soft. Toss remaining ingredients together, spread on Teflex sheets, and then cover with plastic wrap. Dehydrate 1–2 hours, until soft; then toss with mushrooms and set aside.

ASSEMBLY
Place all components on a plate. MAKES 8 SERVINGS, 2 FAJITAS EACH

pasta primavera

Being a lover of all things Italian, I never would have thought I could enjoy a pasta-less pasta. But the vegetables actually absorb more flavor and have great texture. I first did a different version of this dish for a greenmarket class I taught, where I had to purchase and prepare the dish in less than an hour.

SPAGHETTI NOODLES
3 zucchini, peeled and cut to fit spiral slicer
Lemon juice

VEGETABLES
$1/4$ cup halved baby red pear tomatoes
$1/4$ cup halved yellow cherry tomatoes
$1/4$ cup shelled sweet peas

POACHED SPRING VEGETABLES
1 cup almond mushrooms, washed and halved*
Sea salt
Black pepper
Olive oil
$1/2$ cup asparagus tips
$1/2$ cup shelled and peeled fava beans
Vegetable Stock (juice 1 carrot, 1 stalk celery, pinch salt, black pepper)

PARMESAN SHARDS
2 quarts pine nuts, soaked 1–2 hours
1 cup lemon juice
$1/2$ cup nutritional yeast
$2^1/4$ teaspoons sea salt
2 cups water
1 shallot, chopped
2 red peppers, seeded and chopped

WHITE WINE SAUCE
2 cups cashews, soaked 1–2 hours
$1/4$ teaspoon sea salt
$1/2$ cup agave
$1/2$ cup white wine

SPAGHETTI NOODLES
Cut zucchini into thin noodles with spiral slicer. Toss in small amount of lemon juice to prevent oxidizing.

POACHED SPRING VEGETABLES
Toss mushrooms in salt, pepper, and olive oil; spread on Teflex dehydrator sheets and dehydrate 1 hour.

In separate bowls, toss asparagus tips and fava beans in salt, pepper, and olive oil.

Spread asparagus and fava beans in a pan and pour Vegetable Stock over.

Cover with plastic wrap and place in bottom of dehydrator for 4–6 hours.

*Chanterelle or shiitake mushrooms may be substituted.

PARMESAN SHARDS
Process all ingredients in food processor until smooth. Spread mixture onto Teflex sheets; dehydrate overnight until crisp. Break into large shards for garnish.

WHITE WINE SAUCE
Blend all ingredients until smooth in Vita-Mix.

Prior to serving, place in dehydrator for 20–30 minutes at 115 degrees to warm.

ASSEMBLY
Place Spaghetti Noodles in long shape off-center on serving plate; top with crumbled Parmesan Shards.

Pile vegetables (in this order) in front of pasta: asparagus tips, mushrooms, tomatoes, and fava beans. Sprinkle peas on opposite side of pasta. Generously drizzle White Wine Sauce around pasta and vegetables. SERVES 2

baked macaroni and cheese

When I was working with more cooked food, one of the dishes I was most known for was Truffled Macaroni and Cheese. I swore I would never make it again, until Kristen introduced this recipe to a comfort food class she was teaching. I had two servings of it the first time I tried it.

CASHEW CHEESE SAUCE
1 3/4 cups cashews, soaked 1–2 hours
2 tablespoons lemon juice
2 tablespoons water
1/2 cup olive oil
1 teaspoon sea salt
1/4 cup nutritional yeast
1/4 medium shallot
1/2 teaspoon chili powder
Pinch cayenne
Pinch turmeric
1/2 clove garlic
Black pepper to taste

ASSEMBLY
4–5 yellow squash, peeled with ends cut off
Sea salt
1 recipe Cashew Cheese Sauce
Finely chopped walnuts (optional)
Chili powder (optional)
Paprika (optional)

CASHEW CHEESE SAUCE
Blend all ingredients in Vita-Mix until completely smooth.

ASSEMBLY
Process squash through spiral slicer to create long noodles; roughly chop the noodles, toss with a bit of salt, and let sit for 30–45 minutes.

Mix noodles and Cashew Cheese Sauce in a bowl and then spread into casserole pan. OPTIONAL: Top with finely chopped walnuts and extra chili powder or paprika.

Place in bottom of dehydrator at 115 degrees for 1–2 hours to warm before serving. SERVES 4

baked macaroni and cheese

rosemary-garlic
mashed potatoes

This dish is an illusion of grand proportions—you will never know what you are eating or much about it, other than the fact that it is rich, yet airy, and quite delicious.

4 cups peeled and chopped jicama
2 cups cashews, soaked 1–2 hours
1 teaspoon sea salt

1–2 teaspoons chopped fresh rosemary
1 teaspoon minced garlic
2 teaspoons nutritional yeast
Black pepper to taste

Process jicama in food processor until grain-like consistency is achieved. Press out excess liquid with a cheesecloth or through a sieve.

Place in Vita-Mix with remaining ingredients and blend until well combined.

Serve immediately or warm in dehydrator until ready to serve. SERVES 4

Jicama belongs to the legume family and is also known as the Mexican potato and the Chinese turnip. Extremely high in vitamin C and low in sodium, it is available year-round.

portobello steaks

This could not be more simple to prepare, but it highlights how easy it can be to make raw food at home.

4 portobello mushroom caps, stems removed
Olive oil

Sea salt
Black pepper
Balsamic vinegar

Gently toss portobello mushrooms with remaining ingredients. Spread on Teflex dehydrator sheets and dehydrate for 1–2 hours, until soft. SERVES 4

Portobello mushrooms are delicious grilled or baked and are sold year-round. Use them promptly, or store them in a brown paper bag in the refrigerator, where they will last from seven to ten days.

portobello steaks

summer rolls

While a lot of raw food has to be assembled just before serving, these rolls hold up really well and are great for taking on a picnic or car ride. Feel free to substitute other crispy vegetables, sprouts, or different nuts in this recipe.

1 cup chopped Chile-Lime Macadamia Nuts (see recipe
 page 40) or regular macadamia nuts
Spicy Almond Dressing (see recipe page 82)
2 collard leaves, cut in half with ribs removed

1 carrot, julienned
1/2 cucumber, cut into strips
1 yellow bell pepper, cut into strips
Black sesame seeds

Mix macadamia nuts with enough Spicy Almond Dressing to hold together.

Place mixture on a collard leaf and top with carrot, cucumber, bell pepper, and sesame seeds. Roll tightly. If needed, use Spicy Almond Dressing to hold ends together.

Serve with Red Chile–Pineapple Dipping Sauce (see recipe page 72). SERVES 2

> Black sesame seeds are an extremely good source of calcium and also have high amounts of protein, phosphorous, iron, and magnesium.

summer rolls

tomato torta with pesto and macadamia ricotta

This is a variation on one of the first raw food dishes that I ever created. It is great to serve to first-time raw food diners.

MACADAMIA RICOTTA
1 3/4 cups macadamia nuts, soaked 2–4 hours
2 tablespoons lemon juice
1/4 cup water
1/2 cup olive oil
3/4 teaspoon sea salt
1 teaspoon nutritional yeast

TOMATO-GINGER SAUCE
1 cup sun-dried tomatoes, soaked at least 1 hour
1/2 roma tomato, diced
1/4 shallot, chopped
1 tablespoon lemon juice
1/2 cup olive oil
1 teaspoon agave
1 teaspoon sea salt
1/4 cup ginger juice
Pinch hot pepper flakes

MINT-BASIL PISTACHIO PESTO
1/2 cup fresh basil leaves, packed
1/2 cup fresh mint leaves, packed
1/4 cup pistachios
3 tablespoons olive oil
1/2 teaspoon sea salt
Pinch black pepper

ASSEMBLY
2 yellow and/or green squash
1/4 cup olive oil, well seasoned with sea salt and freshly ground black pepper
Macadamia Ricotta
2 roma tomatoes, sliced
Tomato-Ginger Sauce
Mint-Basil Pistachio Pesto
Fresh basil, for garnish

MACADAMIA RICOTTA
Process all ingredients in food processor for up to 5 minutes, until very smooth.

TOMATO-GINGER SAUCE
Squeeze the water from sun-dried tomatoes and discard the water. Process all ingredients in food processor until smooth.

MINT-BASIL PISTACHIO PESTO
Place all ingredients in food processor and process until chunky.

ASSEMBLY
Cut squash crosswise into 4-inch pieces. To create wide noodles, slice each piece of squash lengthwise with a mandoline or a sharp knife to create very thin slices, about 1/16 inch thick.

Layer three slices of squash side by side to form a square, overlapping as needed. Brush sparingly with seasoned olive oil. Spread 2 tablespoons of Macadamia Ricotta over squash noodles. Place a layer of tomato slices over Ricotta. Place 2 tablespoons each of Tomato-Ginger Sauce and Mint-Basil Pistachio Pesto over tomatoes.

Repeat with another layer of squash noodles in the opposite direction from previous layer. Brush with seasoned olive oil, add Macadamia Ricotta, tomato slices, Tomato-Ginger Sauce, and Mint-Basil Pistachio Pesto as before. Repeat steps again to make three layers. Spread Macadamia Ricotta on top of final layer and top with fresh basil. SERVES 4

pad thai

I love the colors in this dish and also the durability of its components. It can be prepared well in advance and easily assembled at the last moment.

PAD THAI SAUCE
1 tablespoon sesame seeds
2 cups sesame oil
1 teaspoon dried red pepper flakes
6 sun-dried tomatoes, soaked in water for 2 hours, drained
2 roma tomatoes, chopped
1/2 cup rice wine vinegar
1/2 cup apple cider vinegar
1 teaspoon sea salt

THAI CHILI GLAZE
1/2 cup cashews, soaked for 2–4 hours, drained, and coarsely chopped
2 cups sesame oil
1 cup nama shoyu

1/2 cup lime juice
8 bird chiles, seeded and chopped
2 tablespoons maple syrup
2 teaspoons sea salt

ASSEMBLY
1/2 to 1 jicama root (for larger roots, use less)
1/4 cup snow peas, julienned
1/4 red bell pepper, julienned
1/4 cup mung bean sprouts
Thai Chili Glaze
Pad Thai Sauce
2 tablespoons chopped scallions
1/4 cup chopped cashews, lightly coated with sea salt and sesame oil

PAD THAI SAUCE
Blend all ingredients in Vita-Mix until smooth.

THAI CHILI GLAZE
Place cashews in bowl; set aside. Blend remaining ingredients in Vita-Mix until smooth. Add to bowl with cashews and mix well. Store in refrigerator.

ASSEMBLY
Process jicama through a spiral slicer to create long noodles. Alternately, cut the jicama into fine julienne with a mandoline or by hand. Set aside.

Toss snow peas, bell pepper, and bean sprouts in Thai Chili Glaze until well coated; set aside.

Place a small amount of Pad Thai Sauce on a serving dish. Top with jicama noodles, and then drizzle noodles with more Pad Thai Sauce. Top with glazed vegetables. Sprinkle with chopped scallions and cashews to garnish. SERVES 4

desserts

One of the hidden secrets of raw food is that it can actually be decadent. Raw desserts are as intense and tasty as any—in fact, I maintain that they are far better, and not clouded by the flavor of eggs and white flour. Instead, they are based on agave, young Thai coconut, vanilla bean, sprouted

DENT, tasty

cashew, and other nutritious and delicious ingredients. Another great thing about raw desserts is their shelf life. Most keep very well refrigerated or frozen, so that they can easily be made in advance. I have to admit that there has not been a day without dessert for me in many years.

INTENSE

mocha pudding

When I first began working with raw food, I made a pudding at home one evening: it was the beginning of many good desserts to come. This is a variation on that original recipe.

2 1/2 cups young coconut meat
1 1/4 cups water
3/4 cup cocoa powder
1/2 cup maple syrup

1/2 cup agave
2 teaspoons vanilla extract
3 tablespoons coconut oil
1/4 teaspoon sea salt
1 tablespoon + 1 1/2 teaspoons coffee extract

Blend all ingredients in Vita-Mix until smooth. For a finer texture, push through a fine chinois. YIELD 4

vanilla crème

Vanilla crème is an essential ingredient in many desserts. My favorite way to use it is in a parfait, layered between sweet nuts and fresh berries, perhaps topped with hot fudge: a raw sundae.

2 cups young coconut meat
1/4 cup agave
1/2 vanilla bean, scraped

2 tablespoons lime juice
2 tablespoons coconut oil
1/4 teaspoon sea salt

Blend ingredients in Vita-Mix until completely smooth. Chill 4–6 hours until firm. YIELD 2 CUPS

an array of desserts

strawberry tart

Strawberry and coconut work very well together—the high water content of the strawberries is nicely offset by the fat content of the coconut, and the combination of the two yields a refreshing, yet creamy result.

CRUST
2^1/$_4$ cups almonds, soaked overnight and dehydrated at
   118 degrees for 24 hours
2 tablespoons maple syrup
1 tablespoon coconut oil
1 tablespoon date paste
Pinch sea salt

FILLING
3 cups cashews, soaked 1–2 hours
^{1}/$_2$ cup lemon juice

^{1}/$_2$ cup agave
^{1}/$_2$ cup fresh (or frozen and thawed) strawberries
^{3}/$_4$ cup coconut oil, melted
^{1}/$_2$ cup water
1 teaspoon vanilla extract
^{1}/$_2$ teaspoon nutritional yeast
^{1}/$_2$ teaspoon sea salt
^{1}/$_4$ vanilla bean, scraped
1 cup extra fresh (or frozen and thawed) strawberries for
   topping

CRUST

Place prepared almonds in food processor; pulse into small crumbs. Mix almonds and remaining ingredients together well by hand. Press into plastic-lined 9-inch tart pan to desired thickness. Dehydrate 48 hours. Chill crust in freezer for 15–30 minutes before filling. If not using all the crust mixture, store extra in containers in the freezer.

FILLING

Blend all ingredients except strawberries for topping in Vita-Mix until very smooth. Pour small amount of filling (about 1 cup) into bottom of crust. Scatter half of strawberries for topping over filling; then pour enough filling over top to cover strawberries and fill tart shell. Chill in freezer 1–2 hours or place in refrigerator overnight.

   To serve, remove pie from tart or pie shell, remove plastic wrap, and top with remaining strawberries for topping. Slice and serve immediately. Keep refrigerated until ready to serve. **YIELD 1 TART**

strawberry tart

agave caramel

Raw food is still new enough that we learn new lessons every day about the reaction of ingredients with each other, and also how they react to heat, processing, and other techniques. We have made some interesting discoveries—among them, we found this treasure.

2 cups agave
1/2 teaspoon sea salt
1/4 teaspoon cinnamon

Blend ingredients in Vita-Mix for 20 seconds. Chill in freezer at least 2 hours. Remove until softer, about 20 minutes, before serving. YIELD 2 CUPS

mocha glaze

This glaze is great to drizzle on a granola bar, tart, or ice cream.

1 cup cashews, soaked 1–2 hours
1 cup agave

1/2 cup cocoa powder
1/4 cup coconut oil
2 tablespoons + 1 teaspoon coffee extract

Blend all ingredients in Vita-Mix until smooth. Store in refrigerator and warm in dehydrator before serving. YIELD 2 CUPS

agave caramel

sweet cacao sauce

Healthy chocolate sauce—what else can I say? Do with it what you will.

1 1/2 cups cacao nibs
1 1/4 cups agave
1/2 cup coconut oil

Blend ingredients in Vita-Mix until completely smooth. Pour into squeeze bottle and store in refrigerator. Before using, place the bottle near dehydrator or let it sit in a warm area. YIELD 2 CUPS

For the raw food community, sweetening ground raw cacao with a little agave nectar is the base for many shakes, smoothies, and soul-satisfying desserts.

coconut crème anglaise

This is our all-purpose vanilla cream, the best sauce in the world for a dessert.

1 cup cashews, soaked 1–2 hours
1/2 cup young coconut meat
1/2 cup agave

1 1/2 cups water
1 tablespoon vanilla extract
Pinch sea salt
1/2 cup coconut oil

Blend all ingredients in Vita-Mix until very smooth. Refrigerate until ready to serve. YIELD 1 QUART

cacao nibs

pumpkin pie with thyme

You will never know that this pumpkin pie is actually made with carrot juice. I think it is my favorite pie—the filling is also great on its own as a cold pudding or flan.

CRUST

2 1/4 cups pecans, soaked overnight and dehydrated at 118 degrees for 24 hours
2 tablespoons maple syrup
1 tablespoon coconut oil
1 tablespoon date paste
1 pinch sea salt

FILLING

1/2 cup cashews, soaked 4–6 hours
1/2 cup maple syrup
1/4 cup agave
1/2 cup coconut oil
1/2 cup + 2 tablespoons carrot juice
1/2 teaspoon vanilla extract
1/4 teaspoon salt
1/4 vanilla bean, scraped
1 1/2 teaspoons cinnamon
1 1/2 teaspoons nutmeg
1/2 tablespoon chopped fresh thyme

CRUST

Place prepared pecans in food processor; pulse into small crumbs. Mix pecans and all remaining ingredients together well by hand. Press into plastic-lined 9-inch tart pan to desired thickness. Dehydrate 48 hours. Chill crust in freezer for 15–30 minutes before filling. If not using all the crust mixture, store extra in containers in the freezer.

FILLING

Blend all ingredients except thyme in Vita-Mix until very smooth. Stir in thyme. Fill candied tart crust and chill in freezer overnight. Remove pie from tart pan, cut into 12 even slices, and wrap in plastic wrap.
YIELD 1 PIE

lemon macaroon cheesecake tartlet

My grandfather's favorite pie was lemon meringue. This recipe doesn't have the added velvety texture of whipped egg whites, but the flavors are all here. It reminds me of those summer days in his kitchen, during my favorite part of the meal—dessert.

COCONUT MACAROON CRUST
1 1/2 cups shredded coconut
1/2 cup cashew flour
1/4 teaspoon sea salt
2 tablespoons maple syrup
1 tablespoon coconut oil
1 tablespoon date paste

FILLING
1 1/2 cups cashews, soaked at least 1 hour
1/4 cup + 2 tablespoons lemon juice
1/4 cup + 2 tablespoons agave
1/4 cup + 2 tablespoons coconut oil, melted
1/4 cup water
1/2 teaspoon vanilla extract
1/4 teaspoon nutritional yeast
1/4 teaspoon sea salt
1/4 vanilla bean, scraped
2 tablespoons lemon zest

CRUST
Mix all ingredients together well by hand. Press into plastic-lined 9-inch tart pan to desired thickness. Dehydrate 24–48 hours. Chill crust in freezer for at least 15 minutes or until ready to fill.

FILLING
Blend all ingredients in Vita-Mix until very smooth. Fill Coconut Macaroon Crust and chill in freezer overnight. Remove pie from pan. Store in freezer. Remove 15–20 minutes prior to serving.
YIELD 4 SERVINGS

cheesecake tartlet

chocolate hazelnut tart

If you have a skeptical friend or family member who doesn't believe that raw food is delicious, simply feed them this tart. Your point will be made.

CRUST
2 cups Chocolate Cookie Crumbs (see recipe below)
1/4 cup coconut oil, liquefied

FILLING
1 1/2 cups cashews, soaked
1/2 cup + 2 tablespoons water

1/2 cup + 2 tablespoons agave
1/2 cup coconut oil, melted
1/2 teaspoon vanilla extract
1/4 teaspoon sea salt
1 cup + 2 tablespoons cocoa powder
3/4 teaspoon hazelnut extract

CRUST
Mix coconut oil into Cookie Crumbs until crumbs hold together. Press in a very thin layer in tart pan and chill in freezer before filling.

FILLING
Blend all ingredients in Vita-Mix until very smooth. Fill cookie crumb crust and chill in freezer overnight. Remove tart from pan and wrap in plastic wrap. Store in freezer. YIELD 1

chocolate cookie crumbs

These are so helpful in a world without flour and breadcrumbs. They keep very well, so make a large batch and use whenever necessary. They also make a great topping for puddings and are good stirred into vanilla ice cream.

4 cups cocoa powder
4 cups oat flour
1 1/2 teaspoons sea salt

1 cup maple syrup
1 cup agave
3 tablespoons coconut oil, melted
1 1/2 teaspoons vanilla extract

In a large bowl, mix dry ingredients thoroughly. Add remaining ingredients to dry ingredients. Mix well with hands. Crumble into small pieces (no bigger than 1/2 inch) onto dehydrator screens. Dehydrate 3 days.

After dehydrating, process in food processor until small crumb consistency is reached.

Sift to separate crumbs from flour. Crumbs should be no larger than 1/4 inch. Store crumbs and flour in separate containers in refrigerator.
YIELD 2 QUARTS (6 CUPS CRUMBS + 2 CUPS FLOUR)

chocolate hazelnut tart

key lime tartlets

This is so tart and refreshing, it's not easy to stop eating! It makes a perfect dessert to finish off a summer lunch of a big garden salad.

CRUST
$2^1/4$ cups cashews
2 tablespoons maple syrup
1 tablespoon coconut oil
1 tablespoon date paste
1 pinch sea salt

FILLING
3 cups cashews, soaked at least 1 hour
1 cup key lime juice
$3/4$ cup agave
$3/4$ cup coconut oil, melted
1 teaspoon vanilla extract
$1/2$ teaspoon sea salt
$1/4$ vanilla bean, scraped
$1/4$ cup lime zest

CRUST
Place cashews in food processor; pulse into small crumbs. Combine cashews and all remaining ingredients in large bowl. Line 4 individual tart pans (or a 9-inch pie pan) with plastic wrap. Press dough into pans to desired thickness (thin is best). Dehydrate overnight. Store in freezer or refrigerator until ready to fill.

FILLING
Blend all ingredients in Vita-Mix until very smooth. Fill candied nut crusts and chill in freezer overnight. Remove tartlets from pans and wrap in plastic wrap. YIELD 4 TARTLETS

vanilla mint flan

The flan-like texture is present in this dish, courtesy of the ever-changing coconut oil. Once it cools, it emulsifies and firms up, holding the dish together. Add 1 cup cocoa powder to this recipe for a chocolate flan.

$1^1/2$ cups cashews, soaked 1–2 hours
$1/2$ cup young coconut meat
$1/2$ tablespoon vanilla extract

$1/4$ teaspoon sea salt
$1/4$ cup agave
$1/4$ cup + 2 tablespoons coconut oil
$1/4$ teaspoon peppermint oil

Blend all ingredients in Vita-Mix until smooth. Pour into plastic-lined ramekins.

Refrigerate overnight or freeze 1–2 hours prior to serving. YIELD 8 SMALL FLANS OR 4 REGULAR FLANS

key lime tartlets

frozen goji berry soufflé

Goji berries are trendy, full of antioxidants, and have a very distinct, interesting flavor. This dish is hauntingly delicious.

1 cup goji berries, soaked 10–15 minutes, blended, and strained
1 1/2 cups cashews, soaked 1–2 hours
3/4 cup agave

1 cup water
2 teaspoons vanilla extract
1 teaspoon lemon juice
Pinch sea salt
1/4 cup coconut oil, melted

Pour prepared goji berries into Vita-Mix. Add remaining ingredients and blend until very smooth. Freeze 4–5 hours. YIELD 4

maca-cacao truffles

Two of my favorite ingredients—maca and cacao—are combined in everyone else's favorite—a truffle.

1 cup cacao powder
2 cups cashews, soaked 4–6 hours
1/2 cup coconut oil

2 teaspoons vanilla extract
1/2 teaspoon sea salt
1 cup agave
2 cups maca

Blend all ingredients except maca in Vita-Mix. Place in freezer 1–2 hours. Roll dough into small balls and coat each one with maca. YIELD 40

warm fudge brownie

This is so rich you won't need more than one brownie, if that; but they are addictive, so it's helpful to consider making a double recipe. And, wrapped individually or in an airtight container, they keep extremely well in a cool place for up to three weeks.

4$1/2$ cups fine cashew flour
3 cups cocoa powder
1$1/2$ teaspoons sea salt
$1/2$ teaspoon cinnamon

1 cup maple syrup
$1/2$ cup agave
1$1/2$ cups water
$3/4$ teaspoon vanilla extract

Mix together dry ingredients in large bowl. Add remaining ingredients; mix well with hands. Line a 9 x 13-inch pan with parchment paper or plastic wrap. Press into pan in an even layer. Dehydrate in bottom of dehydrator overnight. Flip onto cutting board and trim edges. Place on screens; dehydrate 4–6 hours. Serve with your favorite raw ice cream.
YIELD 12

hot fudge

To have a truly hot or warm fudge, I place this in a dehydrator for at least 30 minutes prior to using—it softens dramatically as the coconut oil liquefies.

2$3/4$ cups agave
1 cup raw cacao powder
$1/4$ cup carob powder

$1/2$ teaspoon vanilla extract
$1/4$ teaspoon sea salt
1$1/4$ cups coconut oil

Blend all ingredients until smooth in Vita-Mix. Warm in dehydrator for at least 1 hour before serving.
YIELD 1 QUART

warm fudge brownie

ice cream

Ice cream is an unlikely suspect for a raw vegan kitchen to produce—yet, one of the most fascinating discoveries I have been fortunate enough to experience is that raw vegan ice cream is actually as rich and satisfying as any I have encountered. There are so many variations, it is impossible to stop inventing new flavors. They are also a great way to introduce children to the delicious world of raw food.

mint cacao chip
ice cream

This dish re-creates both the color and texture of the mint chip ice cream I used to find at shops all along the coast of Maine during the summer.

1 cup cashews, soaked 1–2 hours
1/2 cup young coconut meat
1/2 cup agave
1 1/4 cups water
1 tablespoon vanilla extract

1 vanilla bean, scraped
Pinch sea salt
1/2 cup coconut oil
2 tablespoons spinach juice (optional)
2 tablespoons peppermint extract
1/4 cup cacao nibs

Blend all ingredients except the cacao nibs in Vita-Mix until very smooth. Pour into ice cream maker, add cacao nibs, and follow manufacturer's instructions. YIELD 1 QUART

cherry chip ice cream

My favorite—I bring home a half pint every day!

1 cup cashews, soaked 1–2 hours
1/2 cup young coconut meat
1/2 cup agave
1 1/4 cups water
1/4 vanilla bean, scraped

Pinch sea salt
1/2 cup coconut oil
1/2 cup + 2 tablespoons frozen cherries, thawed and chopped
1/2 cup Chocolate Pieces (see recipe page 134)

Blend all ingredients except 2 tablespoons chopped cherries and Chocolate Pieces in Vita-Mix until very smooth. Stir in the reserved cherries and Chocolate Pieces. Pour into ice cream maker and follow manufacturer's instructions. YIELD 1 QUART

mint cacao chip and cherry chip ice cream

chocolate pieces

These are great for adding to ice cream, brownies, or any other dessert that calls for chocolate. The coconut oil gives them a great texture when it cools and solidifies.

2 cups coconut oil, melted
6 cups cocoa powder
1³/4 cups maple syrup

Put all ingredients in a bowl. Thoroughly mix. Spread in thin layer on parchment-lined half sheet pan. Chill in freezer until firm; break into small pieces and store in containers in freezer. Store extra chocolate oil in containers in refrigerator. YIELD ABOUT 1 QUART

ice cream cones

My first job was at a Dairy Joy type restaurant in Maine. I used to love the soft serve ice cream cones, but never knew that I would have a business that prepared them.

1¹/4 cups flax meal
³/4 cup chopped pear
¹/2 cup young coconut meat
2¹/4 teaspoons lemon juice

1¹/4 cups water
¹/4 cup maple syrup
¹/4 teaspoon sea salt
³/4 teaspoon vanilla extract

Blend all ingredients in Vita-Mix until smooth. Spread thinly into 5 to 6-inch rounds on dehydrator Teflex sheets. Dehydrate 5–6 hours until dry but very pliable. Remove from Teflex sheets and shape each round into cones; press edges together. If needed, use paper clips to secure the edges. Place cones on dehydrator screens and dehydrate for 24 more hours until crisp. YIELD 18–20

strawberry sorbet

Simple, refreshing, and light—this reminds me of summer.

1 quart fresh strawberries
¹/4 cup agave
¹/2 vanilla bean, scraped

Blend all ingredients in Vita-Mix until smooth. Strain purée through fine chinois or a sieve to remove the strawberry seeds. Follow one of the ice cream freezing techniques in the Tips on Ice Cream section (see pages 138–39). YIELD 1 QUART

creamsicles

I occasionally have an affinity for American comfort food recipes that are transformed into elegant raw food ones. This creamsicle is a perfect example of that.

Zest of 6 oranges
1/4 cup agave
1 1/2 cups young coconut meat
1 cup water

1/2 cup agave
1/2 cup fresh orange juice
1 vanilla bean, scraped, or 2 teaspoons vanilla extract
Pinch sea salt
1/2 cup coconut oil

Put orange zest and 1/4 cup agave in a container and place in the refrigerator overnight. The next day, blend remaining ingredients in Vita-Mix until very smooth; then stir in the candied orange zest. Pour into Popsicle molds, insert Popsicle sticks, and freeze overnight. To serve, run hot water over Popsicle molds to help the Creamsicles remove easily. YIELD 10–12

almond gelato

Well before I ever heard of raw food, I was an almond fanatic. I first began using them extensively after my trips to Morocco and Spain, particularly after tasting a salty Marcona almond. Since then, I have loved them in everything, both savory and sweet. This recipe uses cashews and macadamia nuts, but almond flavoring.

1/2 cup cashews, soaked 4–6 hours
1 cup macadamia nuts, soaked 1–2 hours
1/4 cup young coconut meat
3/4 cup agave
1 cup water

2 teaspoons vanilla extract
1 tablespoon almond extract
Pinch sea salt
1/2 cup coconut oil

Blend all ingredients in Vita-Mix until smooth. Pour into ice cream maker and follow manufacturer's instructions. YIELD 1 QUART

banana almond butter cup ice cream

This is extraordinarily decadent, given the additional creamy texture provided by the bananas. An alternative for this recipe would be to replace half of the bananas with mango.

1 cup cashews, soaked 1–2 hours
1/2 cup young coconut meat
1/2 cup agave
1 1/4 cups water
2 fresh bananas, peeled

1 teaspoon lemon juice
1/4 vanilla bean, scraped
Pinch sea salt
1/2 cup coconut oil
3/4 cup Almond Butter Cup pieces (see recipe below)
1/2 cup cacao nibs

Blend all ingredients except Almond Butter Cup pieces and cacao nibs in Vita-Mix until very smooth.

Stir in Almond Butter Cup pieces. Pour into ice cream maker, add cacao nibs, and follow manufacturer's instructions. YIELD 1 QUART

almond butter cup

These make great snacks, not just when they are part of ice cream. Keep them in the refrigerator and have them available. They are quite addictive.

1 cup almond butter
1 1/2 cups agave, divided

2 cups coconut oil, divided
1/2 tablespoon sea salt
1 cup cacao nibs

Mix almond butter, 1/2 cup agave, 1/2 cup coconut oil, and sea salt in medium bowl; keep in warm place until ready to use. Blend cacao nibs, remaining 1 cup agave, and remaining 1-1/2 cups coconut oil in Vita-Mix until smooth. Spread half of this cacao mixture on parchment-lined half sheet pan to create a thin layer. Place in freezer for 15 minutes to firm.

Spread almond butter mixture over hardened cacao layer. Then spread remainder of cacao mixture over almond butter; place in freezer until firm. Turn out pan onto cutting board, peel off parchment paper, and cut into small pieces. Store extra almond butter cup in containers in refrigerator. YIELD ABOUT 1 1/2 QUARTS

creamy almond butter ice cream

tips on

how to freeze

These are a few techniques for freezing ice cream creations:

the easy way: Pour the ice cream base into a household ice cream maker and follow the manufacturer's instructions.

the all-day way: Freeze the ice cream base in a bowl in the freezer; every 3–4 hours, stir the ice cream aggressively to keep the mixture aerated. Do this throughout the day until the ice cream is completely frozen.

the juicer way: Freeze the ice cream base in a pan (about 1 inch thick) in the freezer, and then cut into strips thin enough to push through a masticating juicer (such as GreenStar or a Champion). Push frozen strips through the juicer with the blank plate attached.

ice cream extras

Here are some great ways to add extra flavor to homemade ice cream:

extracts: Add flavors such as coffee, marshmallow, hazelnut, spearmint, almond, and so many others to the ice cream mixture before blending.

exotic flavors and spices: Wow your friends with fancy combinations like cardamom and rose water; or try adding lemon grass juice, orange blossom water, or garam masala to ice cream before blending.

mix-ins: After blending the ice cream mix, stir in cacao nibs, dried lavender flowers, raw cookie or brownie crumbles, or some homemade candied nuts. To make candied nuts, chop up your favorite nuts, soak them overnight, drain, toss with agave, salt, and a spice if you wish, and dehydrate on screens overnight.

swirls: After the ice cream is frozen, let it thaw for 15–20 minutes; then stir in the Sweet Cacao Sauce (see recipe page 116) or your favorite strained fruit purée. Return to freezer.

Enjoy!

index

Metric Conversion Chart

Liquid and Dry Measures

U.S.	Canadian	Australian
¼ teaspoon	1 mL	1 ml
½ teaspoon	2 mL	2 ml
1 teaspoon	5 mL	5 ml
1 tablespoon	15 mL	20 ml
¼ cup	50 mL	60 ml
⅓ cup	75 mL	80 ml
½ cup	125 mL	125 ml
⅔ cup	150 mL	170 ml
¾ cup	175 mL	190 ml
1 cup	250 mL	250 ml
1 quart	1 liter	1 litre

Temperature Conversion Chart

Fahrenheit	Celsius
250	120
275	140
300	150
325	160
350	180
375	190
400	200
425	220
450	230
475	240
500	260